Crowds, Colour

Travels in India, Nepal, Sri La

Jason Smart

Text and Photographs Copyright © 2014 Jason Smart

All Rights Reserved. No part of this book may be reproduced or transmitted in any form or by any means, electronic or mechanical, including photocopying, recording, or any information storage and retrieval system, without prior written permission of the Author.

First English edition published in 2014 by Smart Travel Publishing

Cover design by Ace Graphics

ISBN-13: 978-1499610796
ISBN-10: 1499610793
ASIN: B00KFIH8FM

Smart, Jason J
Crowds, Colour, Chaos: Visiting India, Nepal, Sri Lanka and Bangladesh

For Angela, who puts up with a lot

NEPAL
Delhi
Pokhara
Kathmandu
Agra
BANGLADESH
Dhaka
INDIA
SRI LANKA
Trivandrum
Colombo
Kandy
Beruwala
Galle

Contents

Chapter 1. Tea and Biscuits with the Bangladeshi Ambassador 1

Chapter 2. The Pulsing Heart of India 9

Chapter 3. The Shatabdi Express to Agra 31

Chapter 4. Kathmandu 43

Chapter 5. Peaceful Pokhara 65

Chapter 6. Back to India 85

Chapter 7. Colombo and the Elephant Festival...............113

Chapter 8. Kandy Crush..125

Chapter 9. The Slow Train to Galle................................139

Chapter 10. The Beaches of Beruwala 153

Chapter 11. Dhaka, Bangladesh 169

Chapter 1. Tea and Biscuits with the Bangladeshi Ambassador

"You'll be pleased to hear we don't need visas for Nepal or Sri Lanka," I said to my wife, "but we do for India and Bangladesh."

"I'll let you deal with that, then," answered Angela. "What about jabs and malaria tablets?"

We still had two months to go before we set off, but already had much of it planned. I flicked through the folder I'd prepared for our trip. It had sections for flights, hotels and even little pouches for maps. At the back was a special section dedicated to vaccinations. I pulled out our yellow fever vaccination cards and checked them for the tenth time. "They're still up to date, but we need to get a pile of malaria tablets."

Prior to having my folder up and running, both of us had been in a mad flurry of planning, preparation and worry. How should we get from Delhi to Agra? What about travelling along the western coast of Sri Lanka? When was the monsoon season in India? Would it be worth taking raincoats and wellies? Should we fly between Kathmandu and Pokhara or take the bus? Was Bangladesh even safe for foreign tourists? We spent hours pondering these things and more, poring over maps, timetables, guidebooks and the internet; we wanted to do as much as we could in the short time we had. In the end, after testing out different flight options and rejigging itineraries, Angela and I had ended up with a workable plan. We would start in India, head up to Nepal and then return to India before heading south to Sri Lanka. After that, we'd fly to our final destination: Bangladesh. With that sorted, phase two of the work began.

Daily checks on the Foreign Office website to keep abreast of developing situations, especially in Bangladesh, became a daily chore. Of all the places we would be visiting, Bangladesh was the most worrying. The political situation was tense at the best of times, and, with the threat of collapsing buildings and calamitous floods, Dhaka, its overcrowded capital, seemed like a place we should avoid. But sometimes the hardest countries to visit paid out the best dividends.

"I'm not concerned about malaria or yellow fever," I said, putting the vaccination cards back into their special section. "It's the visas."

"Why?"

"You know why."

2

Living in the Middle East was the problem. Unlike in the United Kingdom, where a person could package everything up, send it by recorded delivery to a London consulate or embassy, and then wait for their passport to return through the letterbox a week later, the method in Qatar was less straightforward. In fact, it was a cumbersome exercise coated in full-fat frustration.

The Indian visa debacle was first. With no one answering my telephone calls or even replying to emails, Angela and I were forced into attending the Indian Embassy in person. Managing to negotiate the madness of Doha's traffic system, we arrived at the embassy to find it closed. When we returned a few days later, we were delighted to find it open. We were less delighted when we entered and found it packed to the rafters with noisy people. After fighting our way to a counter, and handing over our visa application forms, we were told to take a seat, but of course, there were none left. Instead, we stood around in the stifling room for twenty minutes until we were called back to the counter, where I was told I hadn't filled my form in correctly. Inexplicably, I'd not put my middle name on it. The man behind the counter informed me I would have to fill in another form.

"Why can't I just add my middle name now?" I asked.

"Because it has already been rejected. Big red stamp across it. You must fill new form in, sir. Wife's application okay though, sir. Hers ready in two hours!"

The room was hot and bothersome, with people everywhere shouting for attention and barging in from all quarters. It was our first taste of India, and one neither of us liked.

"Okay," I said with a calmness I did not feel. "Can I have a new form then, please?"

"I'm afraid that will not be possible, sir. You must fill in the form online and print it out yourself."

"Fill everything in again?" I said, rising. "Even the parts asking about my granddad's surname and what my father's occupation was?"

"Yes, sir. It is the rules."

I looked at Angela. She looked back blankly. I was not relishing another trip back to this God-forsaken place to hand in a form that I'd already filled in once, but now it looked like I had no choice. I turned back to the man. Already, about five people were thrusting forms in his direction trying to push in front of us. "Please," I said, "can I borrow one of your computers so I can download the form? Maybe a laptop?"

The man shook his head. "Not possible, sir. Come back tomorrow."

"But if I'm picking up my wife's passport this afternoon, why can't I give you my application then?"

"Morning is for application only. Afternoon is for pick-up only. It is the rules, sir. Please, I am very busy…"

"Fine," I hissed and stormed out. Angela was hot on my heels. It took me about three hours to calm down. The first battle of the visa had been well and truly lost.

3

I returned the next morning. After clawing my way back to the counter, I handed everything over for a second time. The man gave everything a cursory look, and then told me to return later that afternoon."

"So everything's okay?" I asked.

"Yes, sir. Visa ready in two hours."

And he was right: when I returned later that afternoon, some sparkly-new Indian multi-exit visas had been stuck into both our passports. Phase one of the madness had ended.

The Bangladesh ordeal was next. The embassy was hard to find, hidden in an area of Doha we were not familiar with, but when we eventually found it, we were not surprised to find it closed. Nevertheless, I pressed the buzzer repeatedly until a thin, small-headed young man appeared at the railings. After explaining our need for a Bangladeshi tourist visa, his eyes widened. "Tourist visa?" he asked.

I nodded.

The man regarded Angela and then swung his eyes back to me. He asked us what our professions were, and when we told him we were teachers, he looked even more surprised.

"Teachers? Where do you work?" he inquired.

We told him.

"In that case," he said, "take this." He fished around in his pocket and passed me a piece of paper with a web address written on it. "Download the forms and fill them in with black pen. Tomorrow, come between 8am and 11.30am. And only one of you needs to drop off the application forms and fee."

I thanked the man and shook his hand. He'd been most helpful. As we returned to the car, Angela said, "Well, I'm not coming back. Just so you understand that."

4

The next morning, I was sitting in the waiting lounge of the Bangladeshi Embassy. Unlike the heaving, sweating mass of confusion that had filled the Indian Embassy, I was the only person there. My and Angela's paperwork, photos and cash had disappeared and I'd been told to wait. I looked at the large flag of

Bangladesh on the wall: it was almost like Japan's, except in green and red. Then I gazed at a large photograph of man who I presumed was the president of Bangladesh. He looked like a typical leader: distinguished, bespectacled and with greying hair. He had a slight smile as he stared slightly off camera.

A man appeared from down some stairs, the same man we'd met the previous day. "The ambassador will see you now, Mr Smart."

The ambassador? This wasn't normal protocol, I guessed. I asked why.

The man wobbled his small head. "I do not know, sir. Please follow me."

I trailed the man up the stairs to a door. The man knocked and opened it. Behind a large wooden desk sat a middle-aged man in a shirt and tie. On his desk was a pile of papers, a large fan, a telephone and two burgundy passports.

"Come in," the man said, smiling. "Please sit down."

I walked over to the proffered chair, wondering what had warranted my presence in front of the Bangladeshi ambassador to Qatar. I almost felt like James Bond. After shaking hands with the ambassador, he asked whether I wanted a drink and I opted for a cup of coffee. He relayed this to the man at the door, who quickly scurried off.

The man smiled and looked at my passport. "British, I see? And you and your wife want to visit my country. Tell me, why is this so?"

The man's tone was not unfriendly; in fact, he seemed positively jovial about my presence. It probably wasn't every day a British citizen arrived in his office wanting a tourist visa for Bangladesh. I told him the truth: that we simply wanted to see what Dhaka was like. Then I told a little lie. "It's because we've heard nice things about Bangladesh."

"You have?"

I nodded eagerly, but thankfully didn't have to elaborate because the minion arrived with a tray of drinks and a plateful of digestives. He scurried away again, closing the door behind him.

"Please," said the ambassador, proffering towards the biscuits, "help yourself."

I did, even though I would have preferred a Ferrero Rocher. The ambassador started looking through our visa application forms, moving his stubby finger down through the information we'd entered.

"You are both teachers," the ambassador said, looking up. "A most noble profession."

I smiled but remained mute. I reached for another digestive. They were really rather nice. The man stood and wandered over to an extensive bookcase. He removed a large red ring binder and brought it to the table.

"This," said the Ambassador of Bangladesh, "is my son's chemistry file. It contains notes for his upcoming exams. He is seventeen and I was wondering if you would look at them…and tell me what you think."

I was taken aback, slightly. What did I know about chemistry? I taught eleven-year-olds! But I could hardly refuse a request from the ambassador, not when he had the power of granting our visas. "Of course," I said, taking the thick file. "I'd be happy to."

The notes were full of atomic structures and write-ups of experiments. Headings such as *Ionic Equilibria* and *Transition Metals* made my eyes water. I flicked through a few more pages, nodding my head here and there, pretending to read things I had no idea about. All the while, the ambassador watched me, occasionally sipping from his tea. He took a digestive and nibbled on it while I pored over some diagrams that made no sense. After a few minutes, I closed the file and looked up. "Your son seems very intelligent. His notes are very thorough. He should do well in his exams."

"You think so?" the ambassador said, beaming. "Please have another biscuit."

I did so while the ambassador returned the file to the bookcase.

"You know," he said as he sat back down, "when I found out that a teacher – a British teacher, no less – was visiting my embassy, that's when I decided to bring my son's file to work. It is reassuring to know that a British teacher thinks he is doing well. Thank you very much, Mr Smart, and now let me sort out these visas for you. It normally takes two days to issue them, but in this case, I am sure we can expedite matters…"

As I munched on my fourth digestive, the ambassador picked up the phone and called for his minion. He arrived within a few seconds, leading me to surmise that he must have been loitering outside the door. The ambassador spoke a few words of Bengali to him and then handed him our passports. The young man nodded and rushed away. He returned a few minutes later and the ambassador took our passports, flicked through the pages until he found the Bangladeshi visas and signed them both. "There you go, Mr Smart. I hope you and your wife enjoy your stay in Dhaka."

5

With our Indian and Bangladeshi visas in our passport, it was all systems go. Everything was booked, all flights had been reconfirmed and we had enough malaria tablets to fight off an invasion of mosquitoes.

"I can't believe we'll be in India this time next week," said Angela, reading the guidebook again. She was especially taken with the idea of seeing the Taj Mahal. Since she was a little girl, she had wanted to see the white marble mausoleum. "It seems so unreal."

As the days passed, our excitement grew keener, as it always did before a major trip. We started packing our suitcases and preparing our cameras, but then, two days prior to departure I caught a bad strain of man flu, mixed with a generous side portion of gastroenteritis. The only thing I could do was lie in bed and be waited upon hand and foot.

"Only you could catch Delhi Belly before we even arrive in India," said Angela. Her short supply of sympathy had long disappeared after listening to me moan and groan for a day and a half.

"I'm really ill," I whimpered.

"You don't know what really ill is. Really ill is being in hospital with a drip. Really ill is being on a life support machine. You've just got a cold."

I moaned some more and turned over.

"Just try to get some sleep. You'll be better tomorrow. You have to be; we've got a flight to catch."

Chapter 2. The Pulsing Heart of India

Standing in the queue at Doha International Airport, I felt decidedly wobbly. My eyes were sunken, my stomach was bubbling and my mood was sour. Of all the times to be ill, one of the worst was when cooped up inside an airliner or else standing in a long queue to check in for it. Compounding these problems was the time: it was eleven-thirty at night and the family at the head of our line was hogging the desk.

"Why are they taking so long?" I whispered to Angela. "What's the hold up?"

Angela shook her head but declined to answer. She knew I had a short thread of patience when queuing, and now, with a healthy stomach bug to boot, we were entering uncharted territory. As it stood, we were nine people behind the desk-hoggers.

I looked at the line next to ours. We should have joined that one. The man at the front had just been processed and the queue was shuffling nicely forward. A few minutes later, while we stood motionless, another family in the parallel line was checked in and the queue moved forward again. Inwardly, I fumed as I gnashed my teeth together. I looked at the family blocking us and saw Dad rummaging around in his pocket for something. Mum was opening one of their suitcases, presumably searching for the same thing, and I decided enough was enough. Grabbing Angela's arm, I dragged her into the parallel queue.

"What do you think you're doing?" said a man's voice.

I turned around to face the voice. It belonged to a middle-aged Western man standing with his wife. She was small and dumpy and looked as annoyed as her husband.

"Look, I'm sorry," I said, "but we've been waiting longer than you. Our line hasn't moved for ages, so we swapped over."

"You've pushed in," the man said.

Somewhere deep inside my brain a blood vessel was beginning to burst. It was the last thing I needed: to have an altercation in the check-in line. All I wanted was to get our bags checked through so I could find a toilet to vomit into.

"So rude," said his wife sharply.

"Whatever," I mumbled and then turned away from them. I was not in the mood for niceties, not when there was a potentially explosive device inside my stomach. The man said something to his wife, loud enough for us to hear, but nothing more. Beside me, Angela looked mortified. She couldn't stand it when anybody pushed in front of us, and yet here we were, doing exactly that. The line moved forward.

When we reached the desk ten minutes later, the lady behind the counter looked at me and said, "I think you're in the wrong queue, sir."

Behind me, I could hear the murmur of agreement from the middle-aged couple.

"No," I said. "There are two lines for the Delhi flight, and that one…," I gestured to the still stationary queue, "…is not moving."

"Please don't raise your voice at me," she said.

I closed my eyes. *Please tell me this isn't happening.* I opened them to see the lady staring right back at me. If she wanted to hear me raise my voice then she was going the right way about it because I felt like bellowing to high heaven. Instead, I swallowed hard and forced a smile. "I'm sorry," I said, "It's just that I'm desperate for the toilet."

The woman's glare softened slightly. She nodded and took our passports. A few minutes later, we had checked in for our flight to Delhi.

2

During the night flight, I tried to make myself as comfortable as possible, which was impossible in economy. By the time we were flying over the western fringes of Pakistan, I gave up on sleep and simply stared blankly at the moving map. The pain in my head and the swirling in my stomach were getting worse and, as I shifted from one uncomfortable position to another, I began to feel truly sorry for myself.

My eyes focused on a movie a man in the row ahead was watching. I had no idea what it was about, but my eyes refused to budge from it. At one point, some blood oozed from a tree, and my stomach lurched. I unbuckled my seatbelt, staggered to my feet and stumbled to the toilet. Thank Christ it was unoccupied because, the very second I reached the bowl, my mouth spewed out hot, terrible liquid. *I should be on a bloody drip,* I thought grimly, *not flying at 38,000 feet towards India.* With a grey face and red eyes, I returned to my seat and flopped into it. I told Angela I'd just been sick and she looked concerned. "Maybe you *are* ill."

I nodded and closed my eyes, feeling about as sorry for myself as I ever had. And then, somehow, I fell asleep. When I came to, it was getting light outside. But I did feel a little bit better. It seemed my toilet trip had done me some good.

3

Indira Gandhi International was clean and surprisingly well ordered, which was good because we were both hellishly tired. After clearing customs, we collected our luggage and then found an ATM so we could get some rupees. That done, we wandered over to the parade of men waiting with name boards. My name was on one of them, and I was thankful we'd arranged our airport transfer in advance of arriving. After shaking hands with Rahul, we were led past the trolley boys and babbling taxi wallahs towards the exit.

"How are you feeling?' Angela asked, looking up at the sky. April was the start of the hot season in India, and already the temperature was nudging thirty degrees Celsius. The humidity was bad too, as was the smell – an all-pervading aroma of smoke and wood burning. The air *looked* hot.

My stomach felt tender, and my head was still throbbing, but the worst seemed to be over. "Compared to last night, I feel better. I'm not on the verge of throwing up, at least."

We were soon on our way, and, outside the airport perimeter, the real India came into view. Both of us had seen it on television countless times, but to see it with our own eyes was another thing entirely. India was a mixture of crowds, chaos and colour, with a whirlwind of dust and smoke thrown in for good measure. Roadside stalls selling large and extensive varieties of exotic fruit and vegetables took our attention from the wild and frantic traffic. People were everywhere: shopping for produce, walking in groups or riding on the back of cattle-pulled carts. We passed a family sitting underneath a lamppost. All of them were dressed in rags and barefooted. Squalor was all around.

Rahul, our driver, braked heavily and gave another blast of his horn. A yellow and green auto-rickshaw had just cut in front of us, causing a near collision. From behind came more beeps. High-pitched, low-pitched, shrill and trumpeting: the percussion of Delhi's road system played out a distinctly discordant harmony. It was incessant. Everybody on the road was tooting at the same time.

As well as the auto-rickshaws, smoke-belching trucks, dented buses and lane-switching cars vied for position. We passed an ox pulling a large cart of watermelons and a man pushing a wheelbarrow filled with guava and papaya. Our driver didn't bat an eyelid: just a normal day in Delhi for him. Instead, he continued to beep like a man possessed. As did everybody else.

A road sign read: *Be sane, keep in lane.* I pointed it out to Angela. She laughed. She laughed even more when we arrived at a busy road junction. Instead of staying in the correct lane for turning right, vehicles had come to a standstill in all lanes as they tried to push their way at right angles to oncoming traffic. It was insane.

Rahul laughed. "I think England not like this, sir?"

"No," I answered. "And the horns! I've not heard this many in all my life."

"People buy best horns from bazaar," said the driver, trying to squeeze between a bus and truck. "There is special street in Delhi which only sell horns. For money, people swap normal horn for loud horn. More than hundred decibel!"

Taking advantage of the semi-stationary traffic was a well-oiled collection of hawkers parading past car windows trying to sell newspapers, umbrellas and flags. Less numerous, but more persistent, were the beggars. They seemed to materialize from nowhere and were soon upon us. Women cradling dirty babies gestured for money and street children begged imploringly through the glass. Suddenly there was a gap in the traffic and we jolted forward leaving the beggars behind in the dust and heat.

When we pulled up outside the Oberoi Maidens, we found it to be an oasis in the middle of downtown Delhi. Apart from the occasional beep of an auto-rickshaw, we were in a different world. The only sounds were the squawking of some green parakeets and the occasional outburst from a peacock. We spent the remainder of the day trying to adjust our bodies to India Time.

4

Over breakfast the next morning, I spotted a disturbing article in the *Times of India*. It described the arrest of a gang of kidney harvesters. The gang had been harvesting organs from poor labourers, paying them $1000 (an unimaginable amount to many in India) for a kidney, and then selling the organs for up to $40,000 each. A different article described how a man's conviction of murder (on the hearsay of a dog) had finally been overturned. The poor man had already spent four years in jail. But the most shocking section was the photo of a dead woman. She had been found somewhere in Delhi and the authorities were appealing for someone to come forward to identify her. The photo was gruesome. It showed a young woman who looked like she'd been attacked with baseball bats and knives. Her lifeless head showed black eyes, cuts, bruises and gashes to her chin. Thank God it was in black and white. It wasn't the only horrible photograph. The one next to it showed a road accident victim, the body so badly mangled that the police couldn't tell whether it was male or female. All they knew was that the person was aged about twenty, around five feet tall, of medium build with a tattoo of 'Om' on their right hand.

"How's your head today?" asked Angela as she put down her coffee cup.

I looked up from the horror in black and white. "My head's fine. I just wish I could taste things. It's as if my taste buds have gone. And what's annoying is we're in India – land of curry. I won't be able to taste any of it. Where's the justice in that?"

"I'll tell you what things taste like."

"Thanks."

We finished our breakfast and then wandered to the hotel lobby to wait for our guide.

5

"Hello, my name is Dinesh," said the man in the crisp cotton suit. He was in his mid-fifties, and, like the vast majority of men in India, sported a thick black moustache. "Today's tour will take us to the largest mosque in Delhi, and we will also pass by a busy bazaar. After that, we will see an old Mughal tomb, and maybe stop at something called the Lotus Temple. Come, let us go to the car."

We followed him outside into the blazing heat of another Delhi morning.

The street was busy with traffic, mainly auto-rickshaws. One beeped its horn as it passed but Dinesh waved the driver away. Above us, riding the thermals, were four or five buzzards, scanning the streets for discarded meat, no doubt. Angela and I climbed into the back of the car, said hello to the driver and, when Dinesh got into the passenger seat, set off on our adventure.

"How long have you been a guide?" Angela asked as we joined a main road.

"About twenty years," answered Dinesh. "Before that, I was government worker in the Department of Tourism. Very boring job – sitting in a windowless office all day long. But the hours were good. I arrived at 11am and finished at 3pm. Four hours work a day! The government paid me on time, so I couldn't complain."

To our left was a phalanx of slow-moving rickshaws, the wiry drivers pedalling like mad to make headway, their passengers unconcerned that they were dangerously exposed to faster-moving traffic. We came to a sudden standstill to allow a cow to amble across the road. No one wanted to hit the thing because killing a cow in India could earn the culprit seven years in prison. Everyone waited until it reached the other side, then the beeping began and the traffic moved off.

I asked Dinesh about driving test standards in India.

He laughed. "Let me tell you how it works in Delhi. A person who wants a driving licence will go to a government official and pay a bribe. Then he will get a licence. Simple as that! If, for some reason, they cannot bribe the official, they will pay someone else to sit the driving test for them. This is the system in my country. But there are not many big road accidents in Delhi. Lots of small ones, yes; the traffic is too slow for anything really bad to happen."

I thought back to the photo in the paper but said nothing.

We came to a street so narrow and so thick with people that Dinesh told us it would be easier to walk. Besides, if we even attempted to drive, we would surely kill someone beneath the wheels.

We were in an area of old Delhi known as Chandni Chowk, one of the busiest and most chaotic markets in the city.

6

Chandni Chowk translated as moonlit square. When the Mughal Emperor Shah Jahan (the same man responsible for the Taj Mahal) allowed his daughter to design the square, she incorporated a series of open-air canals that cooled the area in the daytime and reflected the moon at night. The canals were long gone, replaced by a noisy and muddled series of ramshackle alleyways.

Rickshaws, bicycles and men pulling vegetable carts (or carrying bundles on their backs) were all trying to go in different directions. Dogs lounged in whatever shade they could find, and shrill-voiced auto-rickshaw drivers shouted for custom at crossroads. At roof level, thick sprouting coils of electrical cables hung precariously or dangled across the street.

"You want oil lamp? Jewellery box?" said a voice more or less as soon as we stepped outside the car. It belonged to a wiry man with missing front teeth. I waved him away but another tout, this one asking whether we wanted to see the finest postcards in all of Delhi, replaced him. We passed crumbling buildings that overlooked stalls selling brightly-coloured saris and bangles. A cartful of savoury snacks trundled past, and all around was the sound of men hawking up the contents of their throat before they jettisoned it to the ground.

Up ahead towered the huge red dome and minarets of the Jama Masjid, Delhi's largest mosque and our first stop. A high red wall surrounded the mosque, with a large gateway leading to a flight of wide steps. Mobs of people crowded the gateway, most of them beggars, but beyond the iron gates was largely empty. An elderly woman was brushing the steps, sweeping the never-ending amount of dust and grime away.

"You will have to remove your shoes," said Dinesh, as we pushed our way to the gateway. "Angela, you will have to cover up."

We could barely hear him because of the constant babble of conversation and raucous beeping. It was then that we noticed the man on all fours. He was low on the ground, his back contorted into an unnatural angle. It looked ridged and painful. When he saw us, he jabbered something and raised his hand towards us.

"This man is suffering from polio," explained Dinesh, "and I feel real shame that you are seeing someone like him in my country. He is the result of poor education. His parents almost certainly were offered immunisation but because of their ignorance, they probably refused. And now look…"

We stepped past the man.

"But things are getting better," said Dinesh. "The last new case of polio in India was in 2011. So that man will be one of the last we see."

While Dinesh went off to buy some tickets, Angela and I watched a coach making its way along the narrow and crowded street. How it arrived at the foot of the mosque without causing a major catastrophe was incredible. After managing to find a parking spot, thirty or so elderly American tourists spilled from it, most of them covering their noses. The hawkers descended like a swarm of locusts. Dinesh appeared with some slips of paper and ushered us up the steps towards the mosque.

Jama Masjid was enormous. It stood at one end of a huge courtyard, full of giant onion domes and magnificent arches. Around it flew hundreds of pigeons, diving hither and thither until they came to rest on the ground. Their roosting was only for the briefest of moments though, because they would soon be off again, swooping en masse like a magic blanket.

The square was capable of holding 25,000 worshippers, Dinesh told us. At that moment, there were perhaps a hundred, mostly tourists. In the centre of the courtyard was a large pool of water. During Friday prayers, it was where Muslims would wash their hands and feet; today, it was the brief roosting spot for pigeons.

We walked to the southern gate. Below us were hectic narrow streets, coils of black cables and lines of rickshaws. One shop's display hoarding read: *Taj Handicrafts*, another simply stated it provided *Shocker Repairs*. Above them, on a second level, a faded red and blue sign read, *Police Post: Jama Masjid*. We turned to face the mosque again. It looked at peace, a place for contemplation. And then the coachload of Americans turned up and the quiet was shattered.

7

We were back at the car. Stepping into its air-conditioned interior was heaven. Our next port of call was Humayun's Tomb, another big-league Delhi Attraction. Humayun had been the second Mughal emperor, famous for his empire's rapid expansion.

"This journey will take some time," Dinesh said, "so if it is agreeable with you, we can stop at one of Delhi's cottage industries…" He let the statement hang in the air as if testing the water.

"Cottage industry?" said Angela. "As in: small business?"

Dinesh nodded. "The one I'm thinking of is a textile manufacturer – perhaps the best in Delhi. Of course, there is no requirement to buy anything; they will not give the hard sell." He turned back to the front to allow us to consider his proposal.

I looked at Angela and rolled my eyes. Visiting a textile shop sounded like a bad idea. I had no interest in textiles, and, besides, I was sure we *would* receive the hard sell. Angela ignored my face and asked Dinesh about the textiles.

"Mainly carpets and rugs," he said, "and all high quality. They will also offer you a free drink as some refreshments. And me too."

I was surprised that Angela was even contemplating visiting a carpet shop. In places like Egypt and Morocco, people had made similar offers and we'd brushed them off every time. She looked at me and whispered, "I want to go. We need a new rug for the living room. They're bound to be cheap over here."

I said nothing.

Angela addressed Dinesh. "We'd love to go."

Dinesh nodded. "It will take fifteen minutes." He spoke to the driver, who began a turn at the next exit. It took some time due to the confluence of traffic trying to move in four separate directions at once.

8

A young man welcomed us into his emporium of fine textiles with a mighty grin. He led us through a huge warehouse full of rolled up carpets and rugs, to a large room with chairs around the edge. "Please sit down," the man said. "I will get you some chai." He walked off and Dinesh followed him.

I looked around the room. As well as some carpets and bits of rug hanging on the walls, there were a few old-looking machines that seemed to be part of a display. Perhaps the carpet emporium doubled up as a museum. I rolled my eyes and groaned.

"Shush," scolded Angela. "We won't be here long. Just let me look at a few carpets and then we can go."

Our teas arrived on a gleaming silver tray. I took a sip of the milky, sugary chai and deemed it palatable. Angela took a sip of hers but then put it back on the tray. In front of us waited two men: one was the smiling young man who had brought us in; the other was a man in his thirties, who introduced himself as Deepak. Both men had moustaches. Dinesh was no doubt in another room somewhere, being slapped on the back for managing to get the gullible tourists into the emporium.

"How is the chai?" the older man asked. He was grinning insanely.

I took another sip. "Very good."

The man wobbled his head. "Well if you please, we can now look at some carpet weaving equipment. Leave your drinks on the tray. They will be refilled by the time we return." Deepak uttered something to his colleague who nodded and disappeared.

I glared at Angela: *This is your fault.* She pretended not to notice. We followed the man to the old machines. It turned out to be a weaving device. Above it hung an intricately patterned rug. "This rug comes from the Kashmiri part of India," explained Deepak. "A whole family has toiled over it for many weeks, maybe even months. Then they will make another. It is their life. Every carpet they weave is unique."

He demonstrated how such a rug was made. It seemed a painstaking process, involving knots and threads, all using the machine in front of us. No wonder it took months to finish one. After showing us the main whereabouts of Indian carpet manufacturing regions, Deepak led us back to the seats. As promised, our cups had been refilled. We sat down and awaited the hard sell.

9

A new set of men arrived: a trio of beaming carpet salesmen, and Deepak disappeared. Combinations of rugs were laid out before us, with the salesmen watching for any reaction. I couldn't have cared less about the carpets and tried to stifle a yawn by drinking some chai. It tasted like it had six spoonfuls of sugar in it. I swirled it around and the salesmen diverted their attention to Angela who was leaning forward to study the offerings.

Each new rug received a nod or a shake from my wife. The latter meant another quickly replaced it; the former meant it was left for more consideration – the men were narrowing things down quite nicely. After fifteen minutes, I could tell Angela liked the look of a blue carpet. She neither nodded nor dismissed it. It sat there, awaiting contemplation.

"That rug is very special," said one of them, a moustached man with a receding hairline. "Only one of a kind. Please feel free to touch the merchandise. Feel how precise the weaving is. And see here, the underside is just as bright. Both sides of this rug can be displayed proudly."

Angela felt the carpet and so did I. It felt like a carpet, but I nodded appreciatively. I also tried to notice any price tags. There weren't any. Meanwhile, other similar-looking blue carpets appeared. Dinesh appeared too. He loitered by the doorway with a cup of chai. Angela looked at the new offerings, but returned to the original one.

Angela turned to me and whispered, "This would look great in the dining room…"

The salesmen gave each other knowing glances. The balding man said, "It is a very fair price. And because today is slow day, we will accept your best offer."

I nodded, wondering whether we could get out of the carpet emporium without buying anything. It seemed doubtful now, especially since Angela was stroking the blue rug as if it was a cat. And how much was a fair price to offer? I had no idea how much carpets were worth. I sat back, taking another sip of my sweet tea.

The carpet men were waiting patiently. They knew crunch time was almost upon them. The only thing holding up proceedings was the cost of the damned thing. They didn't want to say how much it was, and I didn't want to take a guess. In the end, Angela broke the deadlock. She asked them directly how much it cost.

The man in charge studied the carpet, looking demure for a moment, as if he couldn't possible give us a price for such a fine item. Finally though then looked up. "Seven thousand rupees."

I almost knocked the tray of chai over. Seven thousand rupees was about seven hundred pounds. *Seven hundred pounds for a bit of blue cloth!* I couldn't help myself, I actually laughed. Angela asked me how much seven thousand rupees was worth, and when I told her, she backed away from the rug. She wasn't laughing.

"Okay, offer fair price," said the man with the receding hairline, his smile disappearing slightly. "Remember though, this is a unique piece and would have taken a family many months to weave. It is one of our finest rugs."

"Can you leave us alone for a few minutes?" I asked. "I'd like to talk to my wife in private."

"Of course, sir." When they shuffled away, taking Dinesh with them, I asked Angela how much the carpet was worth.

"I don't know. But it is a good one. If we bought it in England, it would be hundreds of pounds. But seven hundred is too much. The maximum we should pay is four hundred."

"Four hundred?" I spat. "For a bloody rug? We could carpet the whole house for that, and still have money to spare for a few pictures."

"Don't exaggerate. Besides, it will be a family heirloom. Haggle him down to four hundred."

I threw my wife a look. "You haggle him down."

"You know I hate things like that. You do it. You're better than me."

In the end, after much haggling back and forth, we bought the fine blue specimen for £380. The salesmen took our money and gave us an official receipt in return. One of the men wrapped our carpet up into a parcel and promised it would arrive at our UK address within the month. And they were true to their word.

"You got a good deal," said Dinesh as we headed back outside. "You drove a hard bargain. I have not seen one sell for so little in a long while."

10

On the way to Humayun's Tomb, we passed the Lotus Temple. Consisting of twenty-seven giant white lotus petals, and encircled by nine pools, the white structure certainly stood out. Dinesh didn't seem keen to stop, but, after some gentle persuasion, he agreed so we could take some photos.

The three of us stood at the fence surrounding the gigantic white flower. "This temple is a Bahá'í house of worship," said Dinesh. "And is one of only eight in the world. Have you heard of the Bahá'í faith?"

Surprisingly, I had. The Bahá'í religion is a relatively new one, whose core belief is that people should work together in unity, and not be hung up about all the different world religions. In fact, as part of its doctrine, it accepts that every existing religion, from Islam to Hinduism, to Buddhism to Christianity, has true origins and is therefore valid. I knew this because I'd visited a Bahá'í temple in Kampala, Uganda.

Dinesh continued. "It has won lots of awards for its design, and it first opened its doors in 1986. Its interior measures…"

I stopped listening to Dinesh and instead tuned into Angela. Two girls aged about twelve were trying to tempt her with their range of beaded bracelets. They were talking about how pretty the beads were and that each bracelet was worth a lot of money. "No, thanks," Angela said. "I don't need a bracelet."

"But only fifty rupee!" pleaded one of the girls. "I have my family to feed. My brother is starving! My mother cannot work! My father is dead! Only forty rupee! Please buy, miss!"

Dinesh stopped speaking and joined me in listening to the exchange.

"I don't need any," Angela said. The girls were trying to attach bracelets to her arm. She was flicking them away but they were like hounds snapping away at her.

I stepped in. "Twenty rupees for one bracelet."

Both girls looked at me. "Thirty!" they replied in unison.

I shook my head. "Twenty." I showed them the tatty red note with the face of Gandhi on it.

The girls nodded, handed Angela a bracelet and took the money. They sloped off along the street. After clicking a few photos of the Lotus Temple, we made our way back to the car. Finally, it was time to see Humayun's Tomb.

11

Humayun's Tomb reminded me of a red Taj Mahal. It had the similar distinctive dome in the middle, a similar set of secondary domes around the edge and a series of arches leading into the great building. Unlike the white marble of the Taj Mahal, however, Humayun's Tomb was clad in red sandstone.

"It reminds me of the Taj Mahal," said Angela, as if reading my thoughts.

Dinesh smiled. "Most people say that. But it is not surprising – Humayun's tomb was actually one of the inspirations behind the Taj Mahal."

We walked through an archway into the manicured lawns surrounding the tomb, which supposedly represented Paradise. A group of Chinese tourists was following their guide and videoing everything in sight. We stopped at a vantage point near a pool of water.

"So it's a tomb?" asked Angela, a question I was about to ask. "And Humayun's body is actually inside?"

"Yes, but the burial chamber is closed to the public. But you can look around most other things. I will wait by the entrance."

After walking in and around the large structure, finding out it looked far more impressive from the outside than in, Angela and I found a shaded spot to take a respite from the sun. The Chinese contingent was wandering around the other side of the garden, circling a small tomb, this one of an Afghan noble called Isa Khan. They were still filming and taking photographs like mad and I was pretty sure that Angela and I would be on a few of them. Angela opened a bottle of water and took a slug. I did too. It was warm.

"You know," I said, watching the Chinese tourists, "One day there will be some sort of application or program that will recognise any face from a photograph. Those photos they're taking might end up on the internet and you could do a search for your own face and it would scour the web and find them."

Angela took the bottle and put it in her bag. "Why would I want to do that?"

I shrugged. "I don't know. But imagine if it was possible? To see yourself in the background of a photo taken by a complete stranger? I think it would be great."

Angela looked at me as if I was mad, so I stood up and positioned myself in a photo about to be taken by a Chinese man. If I'd judged it right, I'd be standing about forty feet behind his wife and son, smiling and looking directly at the camera. Face recognition software would definitely pick that one up. In return, I took a photo of the man. I returned to Angela, who was shaking her head. It was time to return to the hotel.

12

The next morning we flagged down an auto-rickshaw. I was pleased to see it had an electronic meter. We climbed into the back where I told the driver, who looked in his late forties but was probably a decade younger, that we wanted to go to Connaught Place.

The man nodded but didn't switch on the meter. He was about to set off but I tapped him on the shoulder. "How much?"

The man shrugged. "Busy traffic. Many car! Maybe five hundred rupees."

I started to climb out, and the man altered his price straightaway. "Okay, sir, three hundred rupees."

I scoffed at his new price. According to the guidebook, a journey in Delhi should never be more than one hundred and fifty rupees. I pointed at the meter. "Why not put that on?"

"Not work, sir. Electronic malfunction."

I seriously doubted it. "One hundred," I said firmly.

The auto-rickshaw driver smiled. "Two hundred, sir. Not much to ask for twenty-minute ride."

I looked at Angela and she seemed happy with paying two pounds. I nodded and we set off.

If we had felt vulnerable in the traffic before, now we were skirting with real death. Trucks, buses and lorries were passing with only inches to spare, sending blasts of hot air into our carriage. In turn, we zipped around slower rickshaws, pedestrians and cyclists. It reminded me of being in a waltzer at a fairground, or perhaps a bumper car.

At one intersection, a beggar wearing a dirty red T-shirt approached my window. His arm ended at the elbow and he thrust his stump towards me. I shook my head. The man walked around to Angela's side. She turned away, looking guilty for doing so. When the lights turned to green, we surged forward with a beeping crescendo of traffic.

The amount of rubbish piled up on some streets was staggering. Buzzards and dogs were pecking at it. One family was curled up on the pavement next to some traffic lights. A barefoot boy, aged perhaps four, was playing inches away from the fumes and traffic. A black Mercedes sped past; the driver, a young man holding a mobile phone to his ear, lived in a different world to the street people. The difference between the fortunates and unfortunates was a gulf in India.

13

Connaught Place was a huge circular ring shaped commercial hub with eight main roads leading away from it in all directions. It was bursting with shops, cafes and bazaars. The auto-rickshaw driver dropped us off near KFC and quickly sped back into the traffic.

"Hello, sir," said a voice. We turned to see a young man in a white shirt. He was lounging outside a shop that said it sold office stationery. "You want to buy printer cartridges at best price?"

I shook my head and walked on.

"What about printer ribbons? We have much in stock."

"No, thanks."

A few steps later, a different man joined us. Again, he was wearing a white shirt. "Welcome to Connaught Place, sir," he said. "Are you looking for anything in particular?"

I shook my head and we quickened our pace. He kept up with us. "I can help you. Show you best bargains. Take you to government shop so you will not be ripped off. Many people will rip you off here. I will look after you."

"No, thanks," I said.

He left us alone, but now a beggar woman holding a baby was approaching. To escape her we entered the nearest shop. It was a pastry shop. We pretended to look at the cakes for a minute then left, leaving the trio of bakers confused. The beggar woman was still outside, as were two new men in white shirts. We ignored them as we carried on along the circle of annoyance. The woman stayed put, but the men were more persistent. In the Delhi heat and with the constant cacophony of their voices, we quickly decided we'd had enough. There was not that much to see anyway. "Let's go," I snapped at Angela. "This is bloody ridiculous."

We turned tail, heading back to the main road to flag down another auto-rickshaw.

14

That evening, we decided to see some traditional Indian dancing, or rather Angela did and I had to go along. Entering the theatre (which actually looked like a school hall), I was dismayed to see only eight other people in attendance in a room capable of holding hundreds. And it wasn't as if we were early or anything: the show was due to start in five minutes.

At eight on the dot, a couple of men walked onto the stage and sat down at one side. A collection of drums lay in front of them.

The lights dimmed and a trio of heavily made up women entered. As the men began a percussive rhythm, the women danced. The routine mainly featured hand clapping and dress swaying. Five minutes later, they finished and the ten people in the audience clapped. The women walked off and three more women came on. Their dance was very similar, this time with an added flourish of some bobbing up and down. The accompanying soundtrack was identical though, and I leaned in to Angela. "How long is this supposed to last for?"

"About an hour, I think," Angela whispered. "I didn't expect it to be this bad. I thought it would be that high-energy Bollywood-type of thing."

A single woman arrived on stage next. Six clay pots were balanced on her head, one on top of the other. While the musicians banged out the same dismal racket, she spun and swayed until I was bored out of my mind. Even when a quartet of new dancers arrived on stage, young men this time, I could not rouse myself from my deepening stupor. When a fat man wearing a demonic green mask came on to cavort around the stage as if he'd been stabbed, I could take no more. Thankfully, the demon was the grand finale, and, after the whole troupe had gathered on the stage to bow and curtsy, the show finally ended and we were free to leave.

An hour later, we were sitting in the Oberoi Maidens restaurant on our final night in Delhi. My chicken masala looked delicious but, when I took an initial mouthful, I shook my head. I still couldn't taste a thing. My lingering cold was seeing to that.

Angela was having no such difficulties. She was cooing with delight at every mouthful of her curry. She reached over, took a forkful of mine, and deemed it delectable. "Yours is better than mine. We might as well swap since you can't taste anything."

I nodded and passed my bowl over.

"So what do you think of Delhi?" I asked.

Angela put her spoon down. "Amazing. Absolutely amazing. Even with all the beggars and squalor and people trying to sell us things, it's amazing. So different from Europe. So…alive."

"And tomorrow," I said, "the Taj Mahal. Now that will be amazing."

Angela picked up her glass of wine. "Here's to India."

I clinked my bottle of Kingfisher against her glass. "To India."

Top row: The central courtyard of Jama Masjid, Delhi's largest mosque; Appeal for Identification
Middle row: Lotus Temple; A line of auto-rickshaws
Bottom row: Humayun's Tomb; A man suffering from polio

Chapter 3. The Shatabdi Express to Agra

Our fourth day in India involved a hellishly early start. A man, whose services we'd arranged the previous day, picked us up from the hotel at 5.15am and drove us to Delhi Central Station. Despite the early hour, the traffic was as bad as ever.

The station was another mass of humanity and traffic. Lines of auto-rickshaws waited for arriving passengers, beeping incessantly, their drivers shouting to anyone within earshot. People carrying massive packages on their heads were making their way towards the main building, and we followed them. The closer to the entrance we got, the thicker the crowds became. We were literally wading through a river of humanity. Making our passage even harder were the people sleeping on rags on the ground.

"Come," said the man who had driven us to the station. "Please stay with me and ignore anyone who tries to speak to you. They will be up to no good."

At the other side of some frenzied ticketing booths, we found ourselves on a horrendously chaotic platform. There seemed to be no order to anything. On the opposite platform, a gang of dirty street children were running around, attracting whacks whenever they got too close to waiting passengers. Down on the tracks, rats scurried in the shadows. Worse was on our side of the platform. The dead body was on a wooden cart mostly hidden under a pile of dirty sheets. We only noticed it because of the hand. It gruesomely dangled at the edge of the cart, blackened and charred, while the man in charge of it smoked a cigarette, unaware that his dreadful cargo was trying to escape.

"Here are your tickets, sir," said the man. "Do not lose them. Show them to your guide in Agra. He will put you on the correct train back to Delhi later."

I put them into my pocket, forcing my eyes away from the dreadful cart.

"You will get breakfast on the train, free of charge, and when you come back tonight, you must wait here on the platform. Do not go through gates. People will try to take you to many places. Do not go with any of them. Only wait for me. You understand?"

We both nodded and the man left. Angela was still staring at the hand. We were on our own until we arrived in Agra.

2

The Shatabdi Express arrived with a great tooting of its deep resonant horn. Within seconds, before the train had even stopped, people began pushing forward, causing jeopardy to those near the platform edge. The man with the cart stood his ground, causing a parting in the sea of people. The hand was back under the sheets, we noticed. When the train came to a standstill and the doors opened, a second wave of madness erupted as passengers rushed aboard. Angela and I stood and waited for the scrum to subside and then boarded one of the air-conditioned carriages. Our allocated seats were similar to those found on airliners, even down to the fold-down tray and armrests. They were a little frayed around the edges but otherwise comfortable. We settled down for our first Indian train journey.

At 6am sharp, the train began its ponderous journey through the backyards and shanties of Delhi. Ponderous was perhaps a bad choice of adjective, however, since the Shatabdi Express service to Bhopal (Agra was at the half-way stage) was the fastest train in India. As we picked up speed and crawled through the outskirts, a man in uniform served us each a bottle of water. Twenty minutes later, as the sun began to make its way over the slums and shacks, he served us a cup of hot tea in a paper cup.

I looked outside at the thick black smoke escaping from a couple of tall concrete chimneys, and then at the decrepit hovels that lined the tracks. They were the ubiquitous slums of India, spilling with rust, garbage and scrawny chickens that pecked in the dirt. Men stood at the edge of the tracks, defecating without embarrassment. We passed a group of naked children splashing water over themselves from a large aluminium tub. What sort of life would they have? I wondered as I sipped on my tea. Would they ever see the Taj Mahal or Humayun's Tomb? Would they ever sit in an air-conditioned carriage aboard the fastest train in India? Somehow, I doubted it.

Finally, the slums gave way to open countryside. Lone women tended the verdant fields while stick-thin cattle, and the occasional large, hairy grey pig, roamed about in search of shade. Beyond the big city, India was still living in the Middle Ages.

Breakfast was served aboard the Shatabdi Express. Even though it was only just after seven in the morning, a tray arrived full of fiery hot dhal with a side order of foil-wrapped chapattis. My taste buds were still not in fully functioning order, but Angela's were, and she deemed the curry tasty. I ate mine as the countryside of India slipped past at a hundred kilometres an hour. We had another hour before we arrived in Agra.

3

Agra was another blaze of colour and chaos. Instead of being a tiny backwater village, it was a city of over 1.6 million people. The minute we left the train, a motley collection of hustlers and beggars surrounded us, trying to attract our attention in the noisiest of ways possible. Most were selling the usual tat, others trying to offer their services as guides, but one of the most persistent was a little girl aged about five. In the mad crush to leave the platform, she actually tried to grab my hand.

"Mister Jason Smart?" shouted a voice. A tall, distinguished-looking man wearing a crisp blue shirt and dark trousers was waving in our direction. With his shades and stature, he bore an uncanny resemblance to Morgan Freeman. Angela and I made our way towards him with our pursuers still doggedly in hot pursuit.

Ours being the only white faces had drawn them towards us in droves.

"Hello, sir," said Mr Morgan. "My name is Haris. I hope you both had a pleasant journey." I tried to shake his hand, but one of the touts, an old woman trying to flog bangles, grabbed it. Haris spoke sharply to her, and then to the others, which made them disperse. I wondered whether he'd told them we had leprosy or something.

Haris caught my look. "I told them that there was no point hustling you. I am your guide."

Agra was as hot as Delhi, perhaps even more so. Outside the station was the usual parade of auto-rickshaws, taxis and, oddly enough, camels. The camels were waiting for tourists. A man pushing a large cart of what looked like bright red carrots was passing a large building called the Mughal Bazar: a manufacturer and exporters of goods, it proclaimed. Another man was manipulating a large hand-pump to draw water from a well. Haris led us past the camels, the vegetable carts and the water pump towards a car and driver. "Ready to see the Taj Mahal?"

We both nodded.

As we drove through a narrow street, we saw a man brazenly urinating into the road. Angela shook her head and turned away. I was more interested in the cattle. They were lazing by the side of the road in such numbers that I wondered whether they had escaped from a nearby field. We turned a corner and saw a cow running across the middle of it. Agra was a city of cattle.

There was no sign of the Taj Mahal. For some reason, I'd assumed it would be in the middle of nowhere, visible for miles around. But rather like the Great Pyramids of Giza, which reside within the city limits of Cairo, poking above dusty tailors' shops and cheap jewellers, the Taj Mahal was hidden behind buildings.

The car slowed and then came to a stop. Haris informed us that we'd have to get an auto-rickshaw the rest of the way. "Petrol cars are not allowed near the Taj Mahal due to their damaging fumes."

Haris flagged down a large one, a four-seater, and we climbed inside our third mode of transport that morning.

4

"The Taj Mahal was built by the Mughal emperor, Shah Jahan," said Haris as we rattled along in the auto-rickshaw, "as a tomb for his wife. It took 20,000 workers twenty-two years to build. They constructed it from white marble and completed it in 1653."

"How many times have you seen it?" I asked.

Haris smiled. "Many times. Over five hundred, I think. But it is still magical. I never tire of seeing the beauty of the Taj Mahal."

A couple of minutes later, we parked next to a horrendously chaotic intersection, still with no sign of the Taj Mahal. Haris told us to wait for him while he bought some tickets. As soon as he left, a man on crutches approached. He had no teeth and a missing foot. Not wanting to draw any other beggars, I shook my head and looked at the ticket booth. Haris was already near the front, and how he'd managed that feat was anyone's guess; there seemed to be a thousand people fighting by the hatch. The man with the missing foot loitered, hand outstretched. Angela could barely look in his direction.

Haris returned a minute later. He looked at the beggar briefly but then ignored him. "Okay, we're ready to go. Follow me and stay close. There will be many people pushing and shoving." As we trailed after him, I looked back at the beggar. He was still holding out his hand. I walked away, feeling like a cad of the highest order.

We came to a large red brick structure full of arches and domes. Its tall walls blocked the view of what lay behind, apart from the top reaches of a few white minarets. It was our first glimpse of the Taj Mahal. Crowds of people, the vast majority Indians, gathered by an arched entrance. Instead of joining them, Haris led us to a quieter spot.

"I want to show you something," he said. He pointed towards the main arch. "Look."

We did and Angela gasped. Shimmering in the heat, through the red brick arch, was a section of the white marble tomb. It was unmistakable, and it was beautiful.

Haris smiled. "It seems supernatural when seen through that arch, doesn't it? Like a mirage, almost. The architects designed it that way on purpose. You only get a glimpse from here, a taste of what's to come."

We followed Haris through the archway.

5

Though many have said the same thing, nothing can prepare a person for their first full-on view of the Taj Mahal. Later, Angela would tell me that the sight of the giant tomb had almost brought tears to her eyes, but, for now, in awe of what was in front of us, we followed Haris closer to the tomb, passing pools of water and side channels that flickered with reflections of the Taj Mahal. They also rippled with the reflections of people in colourful saris. The pathways surrounding the great building were crawling with sightseers, us included.

"Notice the minarets," said Haris. "They lean slightly outwards."

We both looked. Almost imperceptibly, they stood leaning to one side.

"They were designed like this in case an earthquake toppled them. They would fall outwards and not damage the great building."

As we neared the main white section, the detail carved onto its exterior became apparent. Patterns and Arabic inscriptions covered huge portions of the white marble cladding. The Taj Mahal was a masterpiece covered in masterpieces. After donning some flimsy shoe coverings, we climbed the steps to a small platform that led to a small, dark entrance. It seemed that a hundred people at once were trying to squeeze through.

Within seconds, we were swept in the rush. Behind me, my back was prodded and poked. I had no choice but to press against an elderly Indian lady in front of me. She in turn was pushed up against another woman. Angela and Haris were facing similar torment. All of us inched forward as the noise and smell of sweat increased. Then, with a final push and squeeze, we were through, into the dark tomb chamber itself. It was remarkably small.

"The real graves of Shah Jahan and his wife, Mumtaz, are in a chamber below," said Haris as we traversed the square room. We were shoulder to shoulder with everyone else, and he was pointing at what looked like two ornately decorated tombs in the middle. "These are just copies. The real ones are closed to the public."

Like the outside of the great building, the interior walls and floor were patterned with marble and decorated tiles. Before we knew it, we'd completed a circumference of the room. "Come," said Haris, "I want to show you the river."

Back outside, from the high walls of the Taj Mahal, we could easily see the River Yamuna. It was a dirty brown sliver of water, flanked by a thin floodplain that bisected a forest of small trees. In the middle of the river was a small boat. Pilgrims sat inside, heading to the opposite bank where, according to legend, Shah Jahan had chosen to build his own burial tomb. It was to be a copy of the Taj Mahal, except in black, but of course was never built.

Despite the crowds, the whole complex was serene. I could see why Emperor Shah Jahan had chosen the site for his wife's final resting place.

6

It was only a short journey by auto-rickshaw to the Red Fort. As we progressed through the thick traffic of Agra, Haris gave us some background information. "It dates from the middle of the sixteenth century, and was constructed from red sandstone brought over from Rajasthan. Shah Jahan was eventually imprisoned there by his son."

"His son," I said. "Why?"

"The usual reasons: greed and power. His third son wanted to be emperor and Shah Jahan was in the way. The son kept him in a tower for eight years until his death, but allowed his sister to tend to him. When Shah Jahan died, he was placed alongside his wife in the Taj Mahal."

We pulled up behind a line of auto-rickshaws. Haris took us towards the large red entrance. Towering battlements, narrow turrets and stone round towers loomed above us. Pestering touts loitered below.

"I'm sweating like an idiot," I said, removing my cap and seeing it stained with moisture. My eyes were stinging with the salty liquid running down my forehead. I dreaded to think what my back looked like. I had felt it dribbling for some time.

"Me too," said Angela. "It must be nudging forty degrees. It's the humidity that's worse."

Haris smiled knowingly, though he seemed oblivious to the ravages of the Indian heat. He had not even broken out into one bead of perspiration. We followed him through the huge entrance, passing alongside one of the old meeting places of the emperor, a white and airy hall full of open-air archways. Further on, we arrived at a viewing point. Over to our right, some distance along the river, was the Taj Mahal, looking resplendent as ever, the haze making it almost ethereal.

Below us, a couple of playful monkeys caught our eyes. They were bounding along a low-level fence, as if performing for the cameras. While we watched them, Haris went off to chat to another tour guide he knew. I looked down at the monkeys and said something to Angela. She rolled her eyes.

"Come, on," I said, "I think you should."

"Let me get this straight. You want me to jump down there, with all these people watching, and somehow catch a monkey and then hold it still so you can take a photo."

"Yeah. Hold it up towards the camera."

Angela laughed. "Why don't you do it? I'll take the photo. I want to capture the moment a monkey bites you and gives you rabies. That's if you don't break your neck climbing down."

"Okay," I answered.

Angela's eyes widened. "Okay?" She looked at me for a few seconds. "Pass me the camera, then."

"I meant okay, it was a stupid idea." I absently swatted an insect flying around my head. I was sure I'd been bitten a few times already. Insects were everywhere in India, I had discovered. We found Haris and made our way back to the arched exit. Along the way, he told us that our final stop of the tour would be a place called Fatehpur Sikri, or Abandoned City. It was about an hour's drive away.

7

"Tell me," Haris asked as we drove away from the fort, "did either of you experience any culture shock when you first arrived in India?"

I looked at Angela. She answered the question. "A little, especially with the beggars."

"Ah, yes, the beggars."

I quickly interjected, "But we both love it here."

Haris nodded. "There is much beauty in India, and much suffering too. But this is getting less and less as the government puts more money into the welfare of its citizens. But I cannot see a time anytime soon where everyone gets the healthcare they need. There are simply too many people, with more born every day."

Fatehpur Sikri had once been the fortified capital of the Mughal Empire. Like the Red Fort, it was built from red sandstone, giving the buildings and walls a distinctly warm hue. Old palaces, large gateways, tombs, mosques and grand pavilions filled up the complex. When British explorer, Ralph Fitch, visited in 1585, he described Fatehpur Sikri as 'larger than London and more populous'.

It was less populated now, and like the translation suggested, totally abandoned. The only people were the tourists, tour guides and touts wanting to be tour guides.

"You know," said Haris, "the third Moghul ruler, Akbar the Great, used to play chess inside a special court here. The game was played on a giant board where each piece was a naked young woman."

"Sounds like a good way to play chess," I said, earning a look from my wife.

"So why did they abandon it?" she asked.

"Bad water. Akbar moved his capital to Lahore instead. Plus, he wanted to be nearer to his enemies, the Afghans."

Thirty minutes later, it was time for us to leave too.

8

The car journey back to Agra took us through more wild and wonderful streets of India. Bare-foot and stick-thin children rushed up to our car window whenever we came to a standstill, some of the urchins laughing and pointing, others simply gesturing for money. Cattle lazed about by the side of the road, fanning themselves from the late afternoon heat with a swish of their tails. Women wandered along the dusty verges carrying large pots on their heads, and, in alleyways, young boys played cricket.

At another jam of vehicles, this time to allow a smoke-belching locomotive to pass, a young man in a dirty grey T-shirt and baggy, wrap-around sarong noticed Angela. He stared into the car, open mouthed, never once raising his eyes above her chest level. With the traffic at a total standstill, the slack-jawed man leaned in closer and Angela didn't know what to do. She looked at me, so I smiled at the man and waved. His eyes didn't flicker, but his slobber did.

In Agra, we passed a Costa Coffee. In the road opposite, a cow ambled by. India was indeed a country of contrast. And then we were at the train station awaiting the great hooting arrival of the Shatabdi Express. It was almost time to return to Delhi. One more night in the Oberoi Maidens and then we would catch a flight to Kathmandu. Phase two of our adventure was about to begin.

Top row: The beauty of the Taj Mahal – photographs cannot do it justice; boys begging for a few rupees
Middle row: The view of the River Yamuna from the walls of the Taj Mahal; The great arrival of the Shatabdi Express
Bottom row: People wandering past the Taj Mahal; Street scene in Agra

Chapter 4. Kathmandu

It is slightly unnerving to arrive in a foreign country under the cloak of darkness. You don't know what to expect, you don't know where your hotel is, and, as you sit in the back of a suspensionless old van, with a strange man driving, it is not such a leap to conjure bad things happening down a dimly-lit alleyway.

The man claimed to be an employee of the Kathmandu Guest House, our place of stay for the next few days. After picking us up from the airport, he had said nothing, preferring to check his phone every few minutes, as if plotting a rendezvous with a shady assailant. Outside was pitch black, the road potholed and uneven, and. as we sped along, my main task was trying to gauge whether the driver was a maniac or not. He certainly drove like one. And his white van didn't help either. If ever there was a vehicle to create mayhem in, then a dirty white van was it, especially if it was a decrepit example with no rear windows.

Ten minutes later, we pulled over next to a line of dingy shops. All of them looked closed. From the shadows, a figure approached, a man. He reached for the front passenger door and climbed in. The driver spoke to him in hushed tones and the man nodded, glancing at us briefly.

"Who's he?" I asked from the back.

"Friend," said the driver. "No problem." He engaged the gear and we moved away from the stores, garnering a few angry beeps from the vehicles behind. I caught a fleeting glimpse of a fire by the side of the road, and then it was gone, eaten up by the blackness. Then a car without headlights bore down upon us on the wrong side of the road. With a beep and a roar of its tinny wasp-like engine, it swung over to its own side and we passed it. Our driver and his friend conferred again. We did too.

"Who is he?" Angela whispered. "I don't like this."

"I don't know."

The van rounded a corner, arriving at a more populated part of the city, thankfully well lit due to the sheer number of bars, restaurants and shops. Perhaps we weren't going to be robbed after all. It was here we caught sight of our first hippie – a dreadlocked man in his forties wandering around in his own personal nirvana. Our van came to a standstill, caught up in traffic, and the driver's friend seized his chance to jump out. He waved as he did so, mumbling a word of thanks to us.

We set off again and then swerved along a side street until we arrived at a car barrier. The sign on it said: Kathmandu Guest House, and, a moment later, a security guard lifted it, allowing us entry. We had arrived in Kathmandu.

2

The Kathmandu Guest House is an institution. A former palace, the guesthouse is centrally located in Thamel (the core of old Kathmandu) and, as well as its free and exciting airport pick-up, it offered complimentary Wi-Fi, things more expensive hotels should take note of.

"This is the most basic room I've stayed in for ages," Angela said as she walked around the tiny space that made up our living quarters. Apart from a bed, an old cupboard and a plastic bin, the room was bare. "And it smells of mothballs. Are you sure this is a Garden-Facing room? God only knows what the other rooms are like if it is."

I studied the tariff on the wall. It explained the complex pricing system in operation at the Kathmandu Guest House. At the top of the list was the Deluxe Room option, then something called the Superior Room. Our supposed room, the Garden-Facing one, was next, and when we had paid for it on the internet a few weeks previously, we'd been charged sixty-dollars per night.

"Open one of the windows," I said to Angela, "and tell me if you can see any garden."

Angela unlatched the translucent window frame and looked out. "No, just a wall. No garden anywhere."

"Are you sure?"

"Yes. Come and look. Unless you count a few weeds growing between the cracks…"

I didn't bother looking and instead studied the list. Underneath the Garden-Facing Room were Standard, Basic and Simplicity rooms. At the very bottom of the list was the delightful-sounding Ultra Basic Room, which cost $4 per night. I looked around our room again, taking note of the mould on the ceiling. "This can't be a Garden-Facing Room. I'm going down to reception."

I was right. There was some sort of mix-up. Our room was a Basic Room. The manager offered his profuse apologies and personally took us to the correct room. It was free of mould, and when Angela opened the window, it had a view of the guesthouse's interior but open-air garden.

3

"You want hashish?" said the small man who approached from nowhere. I brushed him away. We were wandering along the night-time streets of Thamel (pronounced Tam-ell), the tourist district of Kathmandu discovered by Western hippies in the seventies. Narrow alleyways with shop signs advertising traditional Thai massages and trekking tours were everywhere. As in India, the sound of people hawking up the contents of their throats was audible above the din of chatter.

Most of the little shops catered for tourists, selling pirated DVDs, second-hand books, hippie clothing and trekking attire. Other stalls sold prayer flags, glass pipes and Kukri knives, the traditional curved Nepalese weapon made famous by Ghurkha soldiers. The streets were busy, filled with a mixture of Westerners and locals, the latter mainly made up of taxi and rickshaw drivers touting for business, the former a real blend of young and old. In some rooftop bars, rock bands plied their trade; some of them sounding astonishingly good.

Another man approached, this time begging for money, but he was soon gone, substituted by a younger, moustached man. After a quick scan of the street, he whispered from the corner of his mouth, "English? You want marijuana? Golden?" I shook my head. He was gone in a flash, not wanting to attract the attention of a blue-uniformed police officer sitting in a nearby doorway. We found an ATM and after getting some Nepalese rupees, we retired back to the Kathmandu Guest House.

4

The next day we saw a different side to Thamel. Bathed in sunshine, the district was warm and welcoming. Along every side street was a photogenic picture: there a man leaning against a brightly-coloured rickshaw, here a small boy wandering on lofty stilts with a tin cup in his hand. Further on, a toothless old woman sitting on the floor peddling a selection of vegetables, and a painted faced man wearing a long saffron robe wandering around with a smile. We stopped outside a wooden trinket shop where a cow was munching on a pile of biscuits. I glanced at Angela, who looked as amused as I did. Nobody else on the busy street seemed bothered at all.

"You want shoe shine?" a man said. The thin man was armed with a briefcase filled with what I presumed was shoe shining equipment.

"Not today," I said. "Maybe later."

"No problem."

We rounded a narrow corner and arrived at a selection of shops specialising in fabric. One proudly displayed a sign reading: *100% Pashmina! Nepal Quality!* Seeing our interest, a man jumped up and stood in the doorway. "Come in please. I give you first customer discount!"

"Maybe later," I said again. It was something I'd be saying a lot in Kathmandu.

At the next street, I noticed an establishment called the Family Dental Clinic. In the window was a collection of false teeth and a large bowl filled with molars. "I reckon the only qualification a dentist needs here," I quipped, "is a pair of pliers and a hammer." The Family Dental Clinic wasn't the only such place dedicated to teeth – there were half a dozen similar establishments along the same section of street. It seemed most odd.

We arrived at a large plaza filled with Hindu and Buddhist temples. Pigeons were fluttering around tall columns while cows milled beneath ornate fountains. The complex was thick with tourists and hawkers but Angela managed to spot a ticket booth before we were accosted. Two minutes later, we entered Kathmandu's Durbar Square, the biggest tourist draw in Kathmandu.

5

Loitering just inside the entrance to Durbar Square was a trio of painted-faced *sadhu*, Hindu holy men. They wore bright red, orange and yellow clothing draped with flowers and beads. Each man also sported an impressive white beard and long grey dreadlocks. For a small fee, they were happy to pose for photographs. I sat in between a couple of them, and the sadhu sitting on my right laid his dreadlocks over my shoulder. Angela took a photo. We thanked them and stood looking at the temples and fountains. Inside the darkened hallway of one temple sat three women, all making garlands from bright orange flowers. We watched them awhile and then wondered what to do next. There seemed so much to take in.

A couple of local men approached. Both were in their thirties. "Do you need a guide?" one of them said.

I looked at Angela. She shrugged. *It's up to you.*

"How much?" I asked the men.

"Whatever you think is fair," the shorter of the two said.

I hated it when people said that. How was I supposed to know how much a fair amount was? "How about two-hundred rupees?" That was about one pound twenty.

The taller man smiled. "If that is what you think is fair, then we will accept it."

So that was how we procured the service of two men as our guides around Durbar Square.

6

"My name is Sandesh," said the taller man, "and this is Chandra." Sandesh told us that they had been guides for fifteen years. "We met at university while studying to be guides. Sometimes we work alone but often we work together."

"At this time of year," Chandra added, "we might get three jobs per day, but, on others, no jobs at all. It depends."

Our first port of call was the Jagannath Temple, the oldest one in the square, noted for the pornographic carvings on its roof struts. Without our guides, we would have easily missed them. Male statues with members almost as long as their legs were on display, as were smiling gods inserting their members into women's orifices with wanton abandon. And even the animals were at it. One carving depicted a horse mounted atop another.

"Come," said Sandesh. "We will visit the House of the Living Goddess, the Kumari. It is this way."

We followed them towards a wide building. Peddlers selling wooden flutes, bracelets and other trinkets pestered us near the entrance, but their persistence paid off because Angela ended up buying a few items. We stepped into a small courtyard that was surrounded by walls on all sides, the home of the Kumari, Sandesh said. Her abode was three storeys high and featured highly-decorated windows, all of which were either closed or blocked by wire mesh. The four of us stood in the centre of the empty courtyard.

"Have you heard of the Kumari?" asked Chandra.

Angela and I shook our heads.

"The Kumari is a young Nepalese girl who is a living embodiment of a Goddess Taleju. She is chosen carefully based on strict physical features, such as the colour of her eyes and the shape of her teeth. She must have a neck like a conch shell and eyelashes like a sacred cow."

"Yes," said Sandesh, smoothly taking over from his pal. "When enough candidates have been found, the girls go to stage two of the selection process. They each take turns to enter a dark room. Men dressed as demons dance in front of them, shouting and screaming, trying to make the girls squeal."

"Jesus," I said. "How old are these girls?"

"Young," said Sandesh. "Mostly below the age of seven. The current Kumari was four years old when she was selected."

I shook my head. It would undoubtedly have been a good night out for one of the old hippies in Kathmandu; for a four-year-old girl, it must have been terrifying.

Chandra continued, "If a girl shows fear, she is rejected, and a new girl is brought in. Only a true goddess will not surrender to fear, and that is what the priests are looking for – a girl so brave that she will not even whimper. Eventually one girl is picked."

"But before she can take up her role as the goddess," added Sandesh, "she must undertake one final test. She must spend the night, all alone, in a room filled with over one hundred freshly severed animal heads."

Angela looked aghast. "Really? They do all this to a young girl? Why does her family allow it?"

"Her family is greatly honoured!" said Sandesh. "To have their daughter chosen as the Kumari is a great privilege that few people can even dream of. After all, once selected, the Kumari is a goddess. Everything she wants, she gets. She will want for nothing and neither will her family."

I gestured to the building around us. "And she lives here?"

Both men nodded. Chandra said, "She will only leave the house for ceremonial purposes, which is why she is not here today. That is why the courtyard is empty. Usually it is full of people wanting to catch a glimpse of the goddess. But I have a photo of the Kumari; would you like to see?"

Chandra produced a folded A4 photo from one of his pockets. The little girl was heavily made up, with bright red lipstick and thick black eye liner. Her forehead had been painted red with an eye in the middle. Chandra told us it was symbol of her special powers of perception.

I wondered how it affected a young girl's mind – to go through a ridiculously nasty selection process without the support of her parents. It must be a mind-warping experience for her.

"Does her family live here too?" asked Angela.

"No," Chandra said. "And they will rarely visit – it is not allowed. Instead, caretakers will look after the Kumari's every need. The only children she will play with are the caretakers' children, and she will remain as the Kumari until menstruation. Then the selection process begins again."

"What happens to the girls afterwards?" asked Angela, beating me to the question.

Sandesh answered. "They return to their normal life. Many end up married and living traditional lives."

I seriously doubted that their lives would ever be normal again, but said nothing.

7

With Chandra and Sandesh, we had a wander around a few more of the sights of Durbar Square, and stopped at some craft stalls. Angela bought a couple of wooden pots, a large metal frog and two pairs of cloth slippers. When I reminded her that we only had two suitcases, I was rewarded with a look that suggested the metal frog might be used on my head.

The four of us climbed some steps to a roof-top café so we could get a bird's eye view of the square. For a few moments, we stood and gazed out over the sloping roofs, stone temples and rickety buildings. In the distance were the foothills of the Himalayas. The time, however, had come to offer our guides a fair price for their service. Both had been friendly and knowledgeable, showing us things we would have almost certainly missed out had we been by ourselves. The Kumari house, for one thing, was something we'd have bypassed had it not been for them. Instead of 200 rupees, I gave them five hundred each. Not only that, I bought them an Everest Beer each too. All four of us sat at a table on the rooftop café.

"I have noticed something about your haggling," said Sandesh, taking a slurp of his drink. The bottle of beer had a sticker of Mount Everest on the front. "If a shopkeeper tells you how much something costs, say 800 rupees, you should say 250, about a quarter, and then work your way up. Don't start half way. You are being too generous." He looked at Angela. "For instance, those slippers you bought for five-hundred rupees (£8), I could have got for 100 rupees."

The conversation turned to the commonly-occurring strike days in Kathmandu, when public transport ground to a halt, and shops, schools and offices often closed their doors for the day.

"The strikes," said Chandra smiling, "are like carnival day in Kathmandu! People do not go to work and instead have a party. We like strike days, don't we?"

Sandesh nodded enthusiastically. "I think there is going to be a strike in a few days. But only a small one."

"Anything to worry about?" I asked. The last thing we needed was a strike that closed the airport or blocked the roads to it.

"I don't think so. The strikes never affect tourists. The government would never allow that."

After a little more chitchat, the two Nepalese men finished their beer, bid us farewell and went off to find other work.

8

Close to Durbar Square was Freak Street. The street became famous in the 1960s and 1970s as a stopover for hippies as they made their way across Nepal. Hashish shops and cheap guesthouses pulled them in like magnets, and most of the businesses along the street catered for the flowered folk, thus the name. But then the hippies started to make a nuisance of themselves and, even worse, stopped paying rent. The Nepalese authorities grew tired, and started deporting the hippies to India. Then they made cannabis illegal. Even so, the coloured-kaftan and jangle-bangle brigade kept on coming.

But eventually something happened to stop them in their tracks. First, Nepalese border officials enforced a strict dress code for any arriving tourists. If there was any sign of a flared trouser, a whiff of incense or any indication of a coloured bead, then they were refused entry, simple as that. The flood of hippies slowed to a trickle. But the final nail in the VW campervan coffin happened in 1979. That year saw a revolution in Iran and the Soviet invasion of Afghanistan. With both countries' borders closed to tourists, the overland Hippy Trail route was effectively over. They gave up and went to Goa instead.

Angela and I walked down the once-famous street, seeing little evidence of its drug-fuelled heydays. Apart from an establishment called the Old Pipe House, Freak Street looked like any other, teeming with clothes and souvenir shops, and the occasional backstreet hotel. Men on small motorbikes sped by, and a man carrying a huge, oversized cardboard box, containing a fridge freezer strapped around his forehead, shuffled past. Printed on the packaging, in thick black lettering, was a warning. *Do not carry this refrigerator on your back.* We watched him exit Freak Street and decided to do the same thing. We wanted to visit a tall white tower we'd seen.

9

The Bhimsen Tower, built in 1832, resembled a giant white lighthouse, or possibly a towering minaret. Either way, it contained over two hundred spiralling steps that led to an observation deck. At its base, Angela and I wondered whether to climb it.

In the end, we decided to go for it and found a tiny booth near an arched entrance. When I asked about buying tickets to climb the tower, the man nodded and pointed to the price list. Like many places in India and Nepal, there was a dual price rate in operation. The foreigner rate was ten times what the locals had to pay.

After climbing a hundred steps, I was well and truly knackered. My chest heaved and ached so much that I had to stop to rest my hands on my knees.

"Come on," Angela said. "What's wrong with you?"

I didn't say anything, I merely rattled off some raspy breath. My heart was on the edge. It really was. It was pounding and skipping beats. I put my hand on the curved wall to steady myself and then caught Angela's look.

"For goodness sake," she said. "It's only a few steps. You'd think you'd finished a marathon the way you look. Are you so unfit that you can't climb a few steps?"

"Yes," I mumbled.

Angela shook her head, which sprung me into action. I stepped past her, then took another step up, and then did a double step, missing out one level entirely. I passed my wife and took another double step.

"That's it," urged Angela from behind. "Break through the pain barrier."

I took another step, and then a whole load more, with my heart attack edging closer. The pain barrier was not even coming close to how I was feeling. I'd passed it long ago and was now approaching the coronary thrombosis barrier. But with Angela behind me, I didn't stop climbing until I emerged into sunlight. At the top, I collapsed onto a nearby wall and tried to stem the urge to vomit.

"My God," panted Angela, out of breath herself. "You look bad."

I couldn't answer. I was gazing at the floor, unable to focus. But as my breathing slowly recovered, and my pulse rate tipped back down from the red, I actually smiled. I'd conquered my very own Everest, here in Kathmandu.

The view was amazing. We could see virtually the whole of Kathmandu, sprawling out into the distance until it either vanished in the haze or met the mountains. Buzzards circled overhead, riding the thermals.

"Worth the climb?" Angela asked, staring through the wire mesh with me.

I shook my head and then nodded.

10

After lunch, we hired a taxi to take us to a temple complex called Swayambhunath. Once there, we saw monkeys everywhere. Hundreds of them, and none in the least bit shy. Baby ones clung to their mother's backs, adult ones raced along the edges of temple buildings and troops of them congregated on steps, pulling fleas from each other's heads. No wonder the complex was also known as the Monkey Temple.

In the centre was a selection of stupas, temples and shops. Buddhist prayer wheels were in abundance too, and a few saffron-robed monks gave the place an authentic feel. After a quick look around, we found a small temple café and ordered some drinks. A dreadlocked and orange-robed Sadhu holy man wandered past.

Above him fluttered a cascade of prayer flags. A troop of monkeys skittered past, heading towards some steps. One of them deftly slid down the hand railing.

"Remember that shop that sold false teeth?" asked Angela.

I nodded.

"I want some."

I smirked. "Who for?"

Angela explained that she needed some teeth for her class of seven-year olds. She wanted to show them how fizzy drinks could rot a person's teeth, and reasoned that the best way to do this would be by having a real tooth. "I'll put it in a jar and add some cola. Then I'll leave it for a few days."

"Fair enough," I said. I was watching the monkeys. One mother had sat her infant in her lap and was cleaning out his ears with her hand. When she found something, she inspected it for a moment and then popped it into her mouth.

"So can we go and get some?"

I looked at Angela. "Get some what?"

"Teeth."

And so began one of the most infuriating shopping trips ever.

11

We managed to find our way back to the dentist shop we'd seen the previous day. The street where it was located was as grimy and noisy as ever. Even the rickshaws trundling along were making a God-awful racket, their horns sounding like a cross between a trumpet and a dog's squeezy toy. Some drivers used empty plastic bottles as their horns: they were shrill and effective.

Angela went into the shop to try her luck but it was to no avail. She came out shaking her head. "The woman said the teeth were not for sale."

"Not for sale? Are you sure?"

"That's what she said."

I pulled a face. Why would a shop that sold teeth not want to sell any? It didn't add up.

We walked to the next tooth shop. Its window display looked like the gruesome mementos of a serial killer. I wandered in this time, marvelling at the array of false teeth on shelves, in boxes and on display beneath the counter. I went straight up to the male proprietor.

"Hello," I said smiling, showing him my teeth and wondering whether the man was studying them in the hope of harvesting them later on. "Can I buy some teeth, please?"

The man looked at me. Then he shook his head. "No teeth."

I scoffed. "No teeth?"

He nodded.

Surely he wasn't trying to hoodwink me into believing that his shop didn't sell teeth? If he was, then he was insane. Gnashers were everywhere, on every wall, in every space and below him in a large glass case – they were even reflecting off his glinting forehead.

I said, "So I can't buy any teeth?" I gestured at a box of teeth inside a glass cabinet.

The man shook his head. "No teeth."

I shrugged. "Fine." I turned tail and exited the forbidden tooth shop.

Outside I told Angela what had happened. We were both nonplussed. It made no sense at all. Maybe it was because we were tourists, I hazarded, or maybe because they were only allowed to sell teeth to licensed dentists? Or maybe they only sold teeth to people who needed them, and earned extra commission by fitting them? But I was not ready to give up on the mission. At the next dental shop I told Angela to wait outside while I fetched her some teeth.

Like the previous shop, the establishment was full to the brim with teeth: molars, canines, full sets – they were everywhere. A wiry man waited behind the counter.

"Hello, sir," I said, smiling. "I am a teacher and I need some teeth."

The man pulled a strange face while he tried to put these two seemingly unrelated statements into some sort of cohesion.

"All I need," I added, "are two teeth, not a full set. I need them for a science experiment at school. I want to show them to the children in my class."

The man studied me. I wasn't sure whether he'd understood what I'd said.

I smiled again. "Can I buy some teeth, please?"

The man shook his head. "No for sale."

I looked around his shop. If they were not for sale, what purpose did all the teeth serve? It wasn't as if they looked nice – some of them looked old and yellow. It certainly wasn't a museum either. *What did a man have to do to purchase a set of teeth in Kathmandu?*

I smiled at the man again. "But all I need are *two* teeth. Even canines would do it. Please, sir, the children in my class would be very grateful."

"You teacher?"

I nodded eagerly. "Yes, sir."

The man said nothing for a good while, but then went over to his till. After pressing a large button, the tray popped open, but instead of containing cash, it contained teeth. Hundreds of them lay in the separate compartments. Maybe he *was* a serial killer. After swishing his fingers around in one of the sections, he retrieved two thin molars. He passed them to me.

"Wow," I said, staring at the two gleaming teeth. They seemed quite small and I wondered if they had been pulled from a child. "Thank you. How much?"

The man waved me away. "No money."

I thanked him again, bid him good day and stepped outside to hand Angela my booty.

12

That evening, we were wandering around Thamel again. With the light fading across the prayer flag-strewn streets of downtown Kathmandu, I was suddenly accosted by a shoe shiner carrying a small case. Shoe shiners were all over the city and he was the fifth one to approach me in half an hour. Like the others, I waved the man away, but he'd clearly latched onto the poor state of my shoes and saw an opportunity to make a few rupees. As he trailed my side, pointing to my shoes and then gesturing a cleaning motion, Angela suggested I take him up. It would give her a chance to do some shopping without me huffing and puffing in the background.

The shoe shiner was aged about forty, and, like many men in Kathmandu, was small in stature. We quickly agreed on a price of one hundred rupees (60p), and, after sitting me down on the pavement, he began to work.

"Where you from?" he asked a minute later, buffing my shoe with one of his implements. When I mentioned England, he nodded and told me he'd heard many good things about it. "I have never been. I live in Nepal all my life. I married with two children. I had three, but youngest died because we are poor."

I commiserated with him.

"Is hard to live with little money," he added. "Shoe shining is only money for my family." He inspected the inside of my left shoe and found that there was some repair work to be done. He removed a small jar from his case and began sticking small pieces of leather to the inside casing. "This glue," he told me, "is same kind that street children sniff at night. It help them sleep."

The man finished one shoe and began working on the other. He placed the finished one next to me. It looked brand new. Opposite me, a traffic jam had formed and I found myself to be the centre of attention. I ignored the rickshaw and motorcycle drivers staring at me and moved my feet closer to the pavement to avoid their wheels. The shoe shiner declared that the insole of the right shoe was unrepairable and jumped up. "Wait here," he said. "I be back soon." He disappeared around a corner. I couldn't go anywhere without my shoes so did as instructed,

As I sat shoeless, I looked at the traffic. Almost everyone was staring at me. Even a man with a mountain of Styrofoam cups tied to his back was studying me. The shoe shiner returned. He waved a brand-new insole at me and set to work again. The hundred rupees we'd initially agreed upon seemed woefully inadequate now, especially since he'd been working for over twenty minutes, and had acquired a new insole from somewhere.

The man finally finished the right shoe and put it down so the glue could set. As he began to polish the left one again, he spoke. "My mother and father die from drinking whisky. They drink all day and night and when they die, they leave nothing for me. No home, no money, nothing. So now I work all day shining shoe so I can send my children to school. School very expensive for poor person like me."

I decided that when the man finished working, I would give him double the original asking price. After all, 200 rupees was nothing to me, and by the time he'd finished, he would have been toiling for nearly forty minutes. And my shoes had never looked better.

"Finish," the man said proudly. He passed one shoe over so I could inspect it.

I did so, expressing my approval at his handiwork. As I put the shoes on, I decided there and then to give him 250 rupees. Before I could do so, the man asked for five hundred.

"Five hundred?" I said, shocked. That was five times the original asking price.

"Yes, sir. I work hard and buy new insoles. Please, I beg! Think of my family!"

I told him that I would pay 300 rupees and nothing more. The man nodded in resignation. I removed my wallet and found to my dismay that I had nothing less than a 500-rupee note. I asked the shoe shiner if he had any change but he shook his head.

"Well I need some change," I said, feeling slightly guilty.

The man sighed and began a protracted rummage around every pocket and cranny. Eventually, he came up with 120 rupees, which he gave me in return for my 500. All the notes were crumpled and worn, probably the total amount of money he'd made all day prior to meeting me. I thanked him and told him he'd done an excellent job.

Ten minutes later, I was sitting at the Kathmandu Guest House bar with my newly-polished shoes, ordering a beer. Angela was still shopping somewhere; when the beer arrived, I paid for it there and then. Four hundred rupees for a bottle of Everest. I sat back and took a slurp, enjoying the refreshing beer until I realised I'd paid the shoe shiner twenty rupees less for all the effort and diligence he had taken. I felt like a cad of the highest order.

13

The next morning was bright and sunny. For our final full day in Kathmandu, we had caught a taxi to Patan. Once a city in its own right, Patan was now more of a suburb of Kathmandu. Its main draw was its very own Durbar Square and zoo. We intended to visit both.

"These poor dogs," said Angela, spotting another one curled up on the pavement. In the five minutes since the taxi had dropped us off, we'd spotted ten or twelve thin, brown dogs, some slinking in the shadows between the run-down buildings, but most asleep outside storefronts. Further along, we came across a dead one, left to rot with flies. After stepping around it, we spied another dog outside a grocery shop, this one alert but clearly malnourished.

"Give it some water," said Angela. I retrieved the bottle from my pocket and whistled and cajoled it over. It did so willingly, but then stopped at a safe distance. I poured some water into a dry puddle and moved back a few paces. The dog moved forward, sniffed the water, but then ignored it. Angela went into the shop and came out with a large, dry-looking muffin. She showed it to the dog and then put it down. As we walked off towards Durbar Square, we turned around to see it trot over to the cake and devour it in a second.

If anything, Patan's Durbar Square was more impressive than Kathmandu's. It was full to bursting with temples, courtyards, pillars and stone carvings. It was less busy, too. But the heat was too much, so we sought refuge in a café nearby.

"Look at this," I said to Angela. I was pointing at something on my leg, just underneath my knee bone. It was a black dot contained within a small white circle embedded into my skin.

Angela grimaced. "What is it?"

"I have no idea."

Angela peered closer at my growth. "Does it hurt?"

"No." To prove it, I prodded it and then squeezed it. Angela told me to stop.

We decided to visit the zoo.

14

Patan Zoo was the only zoo in Nepal. For that reason, it was popular with families, children and school parties. Because it was lunchtime, most of the children were sitting in rows on a grassy patch eating their packed lunches. Angela and I seemed the only Westerners in attendance.

As zoos go, Patan's wasn't too bad. The animals seemed well cared for, and in good shape. Yes, they had to put up with annoying children making loud noises, and people pointing cameras at them, but, mostly, they seemed happy with their lot in life. We saw hippos, vultures, turtles, monkeys and jackals but we didn't see the star attraction, the Bengal tiger. It was housed in a large enclosure but had hidden itself somewhere. It didn't stop people trying to spot it, though. A crowd was elbowing for position along the high section of wall overlooking the tiger's enclosure. An elderly Indian lady shoved me out of the way with a dig to my ribs. Involuntarily, I stepped back, and another person filled the gap. I gave up and returned to Angela. "I should've thrown that woman over the edge," I said, "and then we would've seen the bloody tiger."

Instead of catching a taxi back to Thamel, we elected to walk. Along the way, we stepped across a bridge spanning the Bagmati River. Along one of its edges were some small shanty dwellings, all of them one-storey shacks with corrugated metal roofs. We could see a group of seven or eight people, probably one family, sitting around a fire in front of one of the hovels. They were dressed in rags but looked happy as hell, all smiling and laughing as they talked amongst themselves. Below us, where the river converged around the bridge supports, rubbish had gathered, including the carcass of some unidentifiable animal. "It's like a toilet," said Angela. "I can't believe this water starts in the Himalayas."

As we got closer to the heart of Kathmandu, the traffic began to thicken and so did the noise and fumes. A long row of motorbikes was queued up along the side of the road, most with their engines switched off. A few minutes later, we saw what they were waiting for – petrol. There was a shortage in Kathmandu.

There seemed to be some sort of demonstration about to start. In the street leading to Durbar Square, hundreds of policemen carrying riot shields and hefty-looking sticks were milling about. In the distance, we could hear a man's voice over a loudspeaker. We walked past the riot police and noticed that the closer we got to the square, the thicker the concentration of officers. They had also road-blocked all entry points to the square. None of them seemed concerned that tourists were wandering in their midst. Some nearby shops were pulling down their shutters and I wondered whether it would be prudent to turn back. The last thing we wanted was to become embroiled in a civil disturbance.

"Hello! You need guide?" said a cheery voice. We turned to see Sandesh and Chandra, the two men who'd shown us around a few days previously. Sandesh smiled. "We noticed you were heading back to Durbar Square. I don't suppose you need a guide again? Very slow day today – especially with demonstration."

"Yeah, what's it about?" I said, gesturing to the policemen everywhere.

"Farmers not happy with government," said Chandra. "Usual thing."

The loudspeaker racket must be the farmers' leader letting rip. He sounded like he was building himself up into a bit of a state. "So is it safe to be here?" I asked.

Both men nodded. "No problem," said Sandesh. "Demonstration will not start for maybe two hours. That is when the fighting might begin. So how about another tour?"

I smiled. "Sorry. We need to get back to the guest house."

Sandesh nodded. "We thought as much. Well enjoy the rest of your time in Nepal."

Angela and I left the men behind and headed to the Kathmandu Guest House. It was time to pack our bags for Pokhara.

Top row: A boy on stilts passes around a dish for a few rupees; Monkeys at the monkey temple; Pornographic carvings on a temple in Durbar Square
Middle row: Me sitting between a pair of sadhu, holy men; Family Dental Clinic – hard to purchase teeth from!
Bottom row: Street scene in Thamel, central Kathmandu; Angela at the bottom of the Bhimsen Tower

Chapter 5. Peaceful Pokhara

The domestic flight terminal of Kathmandu Airport was the domain of smaller turboprop aircraft owned by private airlines with names such as Sita Air, Agni Airlines, Buddha Air, and the gloriously-named Yeti Airlines. Our flight was with Buddha Air and, as we sat in the poky departure lounge waiting for the fog to clear, we came across The Family.

The Family was from the USA. Dad looked the typical mountaineering type, the sort of man who was no stranger to outdoor pursuits. His wife looked the part too, both of them kitted out in the latest trekking gear. But it was their two children who caught our attention most – a girl aged about twelve and a boy of around eight. The girl had just ordered her brother to chase her around the terminal. I raised my eyebrows at Angela. Surely by twelve, most girls had grown out of chase games, but not this individual, because she was sprinting around the room, with her brother in hot pursuit, twisting behind the check-in stands and narrowly missing people waiting with their luggage.

After a few circuits of the departure hall, they returned and stood panting in front of their amused-looking parents. Then they asked if they could play the Spelling Game. Angela looked at me, and we both listened in.

Mum asked the boy to spell 'processed'. He thought for a moment before spelling it out correctly. Dad then asked him to put it into a sentence. There was a brief pause before he spoke. "The man at the airport processed our visas!" Next to him, his sister raised a hand and demanded her own spelling.

"Okay, Alexis," said Mum, "how do you spell 'renaissance'?"

The girl, now identified as Alexis, spelt it correctly, or at least I thought she had. And then she put it into a sentence. "Leonardo da Vinci was a renowned renaissance artist."

Two seats away from this family bliss, I leaned close to Angela. "How do you spell: I am an annoying little bastard?" which made Angela laugh. We tuned out the spelling game and returned to our books. Hopefully the fog would soon lift.

2

Fifteen minutes later, I got up to look outside. There was a whole fleet of aircraft sitting on the tarmac and all of them seemed frail and small. What made it worse was I knew that airlines in Nepal did not have the best safety record. Since 2002, there have been ten fatal air crashes in the country, which is well above the norm. In 2012, there were two particularly scary ones.

The first involved an Agni Air flight carrying 18 passengers and three crew members. The Dornier took off from Pokhara Airport without difficulty, but, thirty minutes later, on approach to Jomsom, in northern Nepal, the weather closed in. The pilots abandoned the first landing attempt, but, on the second, they clipped one of the plane's wings on a hill. The resulting crash killed fifteen people, including both pilots and a 14-year-old child actress from India.

Four months later, a Sita Air flight from Kathmandu to Lukla, carrying nineteen people this time, took off. Still in the climb, the pilots of the aircraft radioed that they had a serious technical issue. Three minutes later, all nineteen passengers and crew were dead after hitting the banks of the Manohara River. Among the dead were seven British nationals.

Angela seemed oblivious to the potential for disaster ahead, which of course was how I wanted it to be. Any talk of poor maintenance or of crashing in poor weather would have sent her racing to the hills. Another thing she didn't need to know was that, in 2013, the EU placed all Nepalese airlines on its blacklist, effectively banning then from entering European airspace due to concerns over their safety.

I sat back down but quickly grew restless. Beside me, Angela huffed in annoyance. "Why can't you sit still for five minutes? You're like a child."

Twenty minutes passed. The American family were all reading from Kindles, Angela was reading her book, and I was playing Candy Crush on my phone. Suddenly there was a hubbub of activity. "Buddha Air 605 to Pokhara," said a man with an unnaturally loud voice, "is now ready for boarding."

At last! Everyone stood up and rushed over to a door where the official now stood. We followed him outside to find the sun blazing, burning up any remaining fog and mist from the valleys. We might actually survive our flight! Even better, our plane looked of higher quality than the rest; instead of a rusting aluminium tube of doom, the Buddha Air plane looked modern and well maintained. Once the cabin crew had closed the doors and the pilots had started the propellers; I decided it was time to update Angela on the safety record of Nepalese commuter flights. Except I didn't.

3

Our half-hour flight to Nepal's third largest city took us westwards. The bus would have saved us ninety dollars but taken ten times as long. For the duration of the flight, Angela and I gazed at an almost endless vista of Himalayan snowy peaks until it was time to land again.

Pokhara Airport was small. After engine shutdown, we all walked across the tarmac into the tiny terminal building. There were no mechanical carousels in use; instead, a couple of men dragged a cart directly from the aircraft to hoist suitcases onto a shelf.

The New Pokhara Lodge was located in an area of the city known as Lakeside, due to its proximity to Phwaw Tal, the picturesque lake that Pokhara had grown around. After unpacking a few things, we climbed up to its rooftop terrace. In the distance was the majesty of the Himalayas, looming heavily over green forests and foothills.

"The air's so clean," said Angela, as we stared at one particular peak known as the Fish Tail due to its distinctive shape. Fish Tail Mountain was over 22,000 feet tall. "And it's so quiet."

I listened. Long gone were the frantic and hectic sounds of downtown Kathmandu. Pokhara was a peaceful oasis of lakes and clean mountain air.

4

"First you should visit the World Peace Pagoda," said the owner of the New Pokhara Lodge, a balding man called Mr Mahendla who, as well as running the guesthouse, acted as a font of local knowledge. "I will get you driver. He will show you around. No rip off, you have my word."

We were sitting in the sunny garden area around the back of the lodge. Mr Mahendla had insisted we sit there so he could serve us some coffee and bread. He was sitting opposite us, pointing things out on our map. "And after peace pagoda, you should go to visit nice cave, here, and then see Devi's Fall."

"Devil's Fall?" I asked.

"No, Devi's Fall, D-E-V-I. It named after Swiss tourists swept in. She die."

Angela looked shocked. "My God. Recently?"

"Not recent. Long time ago. Maybe fifty year."

The taxi journey to the World Peace Pagoda was a hair-raising experience. After leaving the quiet streets of downtown Pokhara, the car began a manic climb up a cobbled pot-holed track full of hairpin bends that overlooked sheer drops into the valley below. Our driver, a thirty-something man called Shriram, seemed to know what he was doing though, and deftly manoeuvred his vehicle around women carrying bundles of sticks, teenage boys leading cattle and vehicles coming in the opposite direction.

The white pagoda was perched at the very top of the hill and we could see it by craning our necks as we jolted upward. It was a large white, cylindrical tower with a spiky golden bit on the top. Ten minutes later, as the gradient increased dangerously, Shriram thankfully pulled over to park the car. "Walk rest of way," he said smiling. "Please follow. I show you."

We climbed out of the car and passed a small open-air café filled with white chairs and a total lack of customers. A man sitting inside looked at us hopefully, but returned to his newspaper when he saw we were not stopping. Some rough steps led to the top of the hill, and on one of them sat a little girl aged about eight. She was wearing a pink T-shirt covered in flower patterns and she moved over to allow us to pass. When Angela thanked her, the girl smiled and asked us for a dollar. Because she was so cute, and seemed to be the only person there, Angela obliged.

The pagoda wasn't just white, it was *brilliant* white. Shriram didn't seem particularly bothered about seeing it at close quarters but told us to go ahead. He loitered by the entrance and lit a cigarette. Angela and I circled the pagoda, and then climbed some steps so we could admire a golden Buddha statue. Buddhas always looked happy, I thought, and this one was no different; with a contented expression on his sleepy face. We walked over to a white-painted metal fence. Below us were Pokhara and the lake.

"I can't believe you and I had never heard of Pokhara until a few months ago," Angela remarked.

It was true. And the only reason we had heard of it was due to a friend at work. She'd once visited Pokhara in the late seventies (probably as part of the hippy brigade) and had fond memories of the place. When she found out we were visiting Nepal, she insisted we visit Pokhara, telling us we would fall in love with the place, which was turning out to be true.

"Look at the mountains," I said, pointing to the north towards the Annapurna range. "They seem so close."

Angela stared a while, saying nothing. Then she absently nodded. "I'm so glad we came here; it's beautiful."

5

The taxi journey back down the hill was worse than the way up. If the brakes failed, the lack of seatbelts wouldn't have mattered because we'd have gone over the edge, plummeting to certain fiery death. But Shriram kept his cool and soon we were back on level ground. "Now we go to cave," he said. "Take ten minutes to reach."

I looked outside at the streets of Pokhara. Stores and shop fronts patterned with Devanagari script were passing by the window. One billboard was in English though: *Make it large: Royal Stag*, it proudly stated. The accompanying picture was of a bottle of whisky. Pedestrians wandered past the stores, as did plenty of tourists. Pokhara was a thriving tourist city, most of them adventurists, using the place as a base for their trekking activities. But Pokhara hadn't always been so tourist-friendly.

Following China's annexation of Tibet in the 1960s, the once busy trade route from Tibet to India (which passed through Pokhara) died. Pokhara almost did too, especially since the town was only accessible by foot or from a small landing strip. Its resurgence came about, partly, because of trailblazing hippies who stumbled upon it. It was like a haven for them, somewhere away from the prying eyes of the authorities where they could live among mountain flowers in peace. A small service industry grew up around the hippies, powered by local Nepalese workers. As the town's population grew, so did its economy, and then somebody decided to build a road connecting it to Kathmandu. People could now travel to Pokhara by bus, and they did so in great numbers. Pokhara thrived. Nowadays, trekkers have replaced the hippies, and their presence provides much-needed jobs for the local community.

Shriram pulled up by a busy street. I wondered why we'd stopped because there was no cave in sight, unless he wanted to show us a tourist tat shop first, of which there were plenty. He told us to follow him, and we did so, weaving between the shops and waving proprietors until we arrived at a cave entrance hidden at the end of a track. We were the only people there.

Inside the opening, our eyes adjusted to the dark and swiftly discovered there wasn't much to see. A few dim light bulbs illuminated a rocky trail and the rickety iron fence running along one side of the cave, there to stop errant hikers from tumbling over the edge. Apart from the dank-looking cave ceiling, that was it: nothing. Shriram led us along the trail and we followed, gripping the handrail to stop us slipping on the damp stones beneath our feet.

I turned to Angela, and even in the faint light, I could see her expression was not favourable. The cave was an empty cavern without even a single stalactite to keep us interested. The only thing of note was the constant crashing of water from somewhere. After a few metres, Shriram stopped. In front of him was a narrower section of the cave, one that would involve stooping, shimmying and perhaps even limbo dancing. "You want to carry on?" he asked.

I looked at Angela. She shrugged. "What else is there to see?" she asked.

Shriram looked confused. "More cave."

We decided to go back. It was only later we discovered that if we had carried on, we would've seen a massive stalactite that people worshipped as Shiva. Instead, we retraced our steps out of the cave, ambled past the tat shops and then crossed over a main road. On the other side was the entrance to Devi's Fall. Once again, we were the only people there.

6

Shriram led us on a short hike across some limestone-littered terrain until we came to a gushing stream that had cut through the soft rock to create a sort of gulley. He stopped and gestured that we should look down. He lit a cigarette and sat down on a rock. Angela and I walked to the edge and stared. I hadn't been expecting Victoria Falls, but this was pretty bad. Instead of a white-water torrent, Devi's Fall was a weak cascade of water, dribbling out from some moss-covered rocks. I leaned towards my wife so that Shriram wouldn't hear. "This is rubbish," I whispered. "I've seen hose pipes with more power."

Angela laughed. "I reckon the only reason this place is famous is because of that woman who died. They've created something out of nothing."

"God knows how she was swept away in that…?"

While Shriram finished his cigarette, we walked a little further downstream. Despite the lack of torrential torrents, it was still a fairly picturesque place. In England, it would be the perfect spot for a picnic, or maybe a lovers' retreat.

I looked down at my knee. My growth had enlarged since Angela had last seen it, and was now about half a centimetre in diameter with a milky white glow. The most curious thing was the black dot in the centre. At first I thought it might be a splinter, but splinters usually hurt when you pressed them. This didn't, and the white section felt hard too, like a piece of plastic. Even when I pulled or twisted it, there was no pain. I wondered whether it could be an insect bite.

Angela peered at it again. "It's disgusting."

I nodded and prodded it. Angela looked away.

We glanced over at Shriram, but he was busy speaking into his phone. Angela told me to leave my growth alone. I did, and we turned around to let Shriram know we were done. He nodded and finished his conversation. Soon we were back at the New Pokhara Lodge after a successful jaunt to see the sights of the city.

7

The next morning, the alarm clock chimed into dreadful life at the ungodly hour of 5am. My dream of crashing cascades and dank crevices was shattered in the space of two nasty seconds. Angela was already up, peering behind the curtains. It was dark outside. "Come on, get up."

"We're on holiday," I croaked. "Let me sleep."

My wife ignored me, opening the window to take in some fresh mountain air.

The previous day, Shriram had suggested we might enjoy an early morning hike up to the village of Sarankot so we could watch a Himalayan sunrise. He promised we would see a wonderful phenomenon – the mountains turning pink. Angela was immediately sold, and somehow she convinced me that it would be a good idea too, but at 5am, before even the roosters had awakened, I couldn't think of anything worse.

Half an hour later, Shriram was waiting outside in his taxi. His headlights were on, and they were the only source of light in the street. I took a moment's glee that he looked more knackered than I did. The main streets of Pokhara were just as dark as the side streets. Shriram was constantly beeping to warn other road users (cyclists, pedestrians and cows) that we were coming their way. Sometime later, we left the main road and turned onto a track that only four-wheel drives should have been allowed on. As we weaved our way up the mountain, I could smell the taxi's clutch burning in agony.

I wondered how often Shriram did the trip. He wasn't exactly overweight, but he certainly wasn't agile looking. Indeed, on the walk up to the World Peace Pagoda, he had been more out of breath than me. At least he looked awake now, concentrating fully on where he was going. After another few twists and turns, we arrived at a plateau of sorts, and Shriram pulled over and parked next to a few other vehicles. Some of them were emptying out their passengers: all young and fit-looking westerners. The sunrise hike to Sarankot village was evidently a popular one.

"Stay in car," said Shriram. "I go find guide."

Aha! I thought. Shriram was a clever sod, after all! While we went off with a guide up the mountain, he could recline his seat, have a snooze, and then, an hour later, drive us back to the guesthouse. A master plan if ever there was one. Shriram returned with a young Nepalese man in tow. Angela and I got out of the car to say hello.

"Hi, my name is Lagan," the newcomer said in clear and remarkably good English. He was wearing an Adidas jacket and a white woolly hat.

I commented on Lagan's good English.

"Wow, thanks. I'm actually studying management at Pokhara University, but every morning I earn some extra money as a guide. I watch lots of American DVDs too."

It was time to set off.

8

Though still dark, sunrise was less than an hour away. Lagan bounded up some steep stone steps and we followed on after him, still feeling the chill in the pre-dawn air. Ten minutes later, we arrived at a cliff face. A set of plastic chairs overlooked the valley. Out in the distance, we could make out the shadows of the Himalayas.

"You have a choice," said our young guide. "You can stay here for the sunrise, or we can climb to the top and watch it from there. There is no real difference in the view but perhaps you want a good hike?"

I looked at the chairs and could see myself sitting in one of them, perhaps drinking a cup of tea as I removed the chill from my bones. I was about to claim one when Angela stopped me in my tracks. "We'd like to go the top, please," she announced.

I shot her a glance of annoyance, but she ignored it. Lagan nodded and bounded off again, with Angela close behind. Within a minute, I was panting and wheezing like an old man, trying to keep up. But somehow I did, and took solace in the fact that we seemed to be the fastest group on the trail. I quickly lost count of the number of people we passed.

Soon, however, I reached a point where the pain became too much. My lungs were on fire, and every breath was bringing a worrying pain to my throat. Lagan came down to see me. He looked as fit as a fiddle. "Mr Jason," he said, "not far to the top. But we need to keep up the pace or else we may miss the sunrise. All these people we are passing will miss it, I'm sure, but not us. Just a few more minutes. Do you think you can carry on?"

I nodded and forced myself on. How could I not? Up along the steep upwards trail the three of us went, passing locals setting up stalls or carrying bundles of straw. I passed a tin-roofed shed with a cow inside munching on some grass, and then, further up, I said hello to an elderly woman collecting water from a pipe in a large jug. Very soon, my chest and thighs were in agony again, and, with all thoughts of comfortable chairs gone, my delirious mind turned to helicopters and Medivac personnel. And then, quite miraculously, we reached the top. I experienced what Sir Edmund Hillary must have felt when he'd scaled Everest. All I needed was a flag and an oxygen mask.

9

We joined the other twenty or so people who had also made it. "When the sun rises, the peaks will turn pink," said Lagan. "You will take many great photos. And it is good that we arrived so early; we can get the best vantage point."

He took us to one of the highest places on the plateau. The sun was on the move over a distant horizon and, little by little, almost imperceptibly, the landscape turned from black to grey, then blue to red. In the distance, smoke lazily drifted from a few shacks on the hillsides, but, apart from that, everything was still and quiet.

"Are you glad you did it now?" asked Angela.

"I'm not sure. It looks the same as it did near the chairs."

Angela shook her head. "But now we can appreciate the view more."

"My head feels like I've had a thousand vodkas. My innards feel like they've done a round with Muhammad Ali. My legs feel like—"

"Stop exaggerating."

Lagan pointed at a settlement down in a deep valley below. "That is Tibetan refugee camp. After the exile of the Dalai Lama, thousands of Tibetans arrived in Nepal. Most moved on to India, but many stayed. It is one of twelve such camps in my country. If you have time, you can visit it from Pokhara. Maybe to buy handicrafts and other such things."

By now, the valley was lighting up and everyone was staring at the line of jagged peaks in front of us. They *were* turning pink, albeit with an orange tint, and cameras were going off everywhere. As the sun came up further, the pink dissipated, and, fifteen minutes later, they looked like regular daytime mountains, and so it was time to head back down. On the way, I realised how much of a weakling I was. Old women were walking up the trail carrying large bundles supported by bands around their foreheads. Children were running up laughing and giggling, calling out *Namaste*, the customary greeting, to everyone they passed. We arrived back at Shriram's car uplifted by our experience. He looked like he'd just woken up.

10

Phewa Lake is the main tourist draw in Pokhara. Guest houses, restaurants, gift shops, trekking stores and barber shacks line one edge of it. Whenever Angela and I passed one of the barber's shacks, a man would jump up and ask whether I needed a shave.

"You are looking a bit rugged," said Angela. "You could actually pass for a trekker, until you step foot on a mountain, that is. Then you become a pathetic whinger."

"Thanks."

The street running parallel to the lake was quiet, apart from a trio of cows trotting along the middle, accompanied by a stray dog that was keeping up with them on the pavement. All four slowed near a wheeled cart that had labelled itself the *Sausage Centre*. Why it was called that, we couldn't tell, because, as far as we could see, it only sold fresh orange juice. As strange as that was, there was something even odder. When Angela spotted it, her eyes widened.

The bizarre vehicle looked like it had been bastardised from four or five different things. A small tractor engine powered the contraption – and, if ever a vehicle deserved the term contraption, this was it – and holding the engine above the ground were a couple of small, threadbare wheels. Then a narrow beam of metal led from the engine section towards the open-air seating compartment. The driver had to rest his feet on the beam or else they would drag on the floor. His passenger sat alongside him, keeping his feet crossed and raised, dangling over thin air, while above their heads, the maker of the jalopy had slung a piece of green tarpaulin around a loose metal frame. Behind the cab was a trailer where a third man sat amid boxes, bundles and what looked like a picture frame. When the vehicle set off, our eyes were drawn to its method of turning. Instead of a steering wheel, the driver manhandled long, fork-like handlebars (similar to a Harley Davidson) connected to the front wheels. With a belch of smoke and a crack of a misfiring engine, it trundled off down the street. No one else batted an eyelid.

11

The other side of the lake was made up of forested highland where monkeys apparently roamed in abundance. We were too far away to tell if any were there, so instead stopped by the shore next to a few rowing boats. It took about thirty seconds for a teenage boat tout to rush over. For next to nothing, we were able to secure the use of a small blue boat for one hour.

Having completed a basic canoeing course, aged ten, and being a rugged outdoor trekker, I took control of the oars first. I soon had us out into the calm blue expanse of the lake. Apart from a few boats near a tiny island in the middle, we had the whole place to ourselves.

"It's so peaceful," commented Angela. "Just look at the view." I swivelled my head and stopped rowing. My arms were aching and so was my back. I'd exceeded my exercise quota for the month in just one day. In the far distance, above a line of trees, was the mountain range we'd seen earlier.

Angela said, "Why have you stopped rowing? The breeze was really nice."

"Sorry, your majesty. I just wanted to catch a morsel of breath. We shall set forth soon."

"Good. And put some welly into it next time."

I decided to investigate the island. It seemed to house some sort of temple. I turned the boat around and began to row full steam ahead towards it.

"Where are we going?"

"To the island, if it pleases you."

"It does. Faster!" ordered Angela.

I pulled a face and Angela laughed, but soon enough we arrived at the island, and I brought the boat to a stop next to a series of red and white steps covered with pigeons. It was then I realised we had no way of tying our boat up. Angela didn't seem overly concerned about the temple, anyway – she was more bothered about catching the sun – so I used one of the oars to push ourselves away from the side, and then rowed us on a slow journey past the forests on the far edge (we didn't see any monkeys) before returning our boat to its starting place.

"Right," announced Angela when we'd parked our ship, "I'm going for a massage at Seeing Hands. It'll take about an hour. You can either go back to the guesthouse or find a bar and have a drink. Either way, I'll text you when I've finished." Seeing Hands was an establishment staffed by blind masseurs. It was a lifeline because it gave many blind people a chance to earn an income rather than having to beg for money. Additionally, part of the fee was used to train future masseurs.

I told Angela I'd go for a drink.

12

The bar I chose was on the main lake street and had a seating area in an upstairs, open-air veranda. I ordered a Diet Coke and looked down at the life going on below me. Men on bicycles made up most of the traffic, but there were more than enough thin motorbikes zipping along to shatter any semblance of peace. Perhaps because it was lunchtime, the juice stalls were doing brisk business, as were the tourist shops selling ponchos and carved wooden masks. The Sausage Centre had moved on, I noticed.

A couple of beggars caught my eye. They were a husband and wife team in their late seventies. The man was blind and his wife was leading him by his hand. In her other hand, she carried a short stick. They were shuffling past every bar and cafe, stopping at each to beg for a few rupees.

My ice-cold drink was just what the doctor ordered after the strenuous activity of the day. I took another sip and thought about how lucky Angela and I were. The previous week we had been gazing at the Taj Mahal, and now we were in one of the most beautiful cities ever. And we still had so much more to see on our trip.

Forty minutes later, Angela joined me on the veranda. I asked her about the massage.

"Really good," she beamed. "The woman was so strong. She really worked on the knots in my back."

"Are you sure it was a woman?" I asked.

"What do you mean? Of course she was a woman. How could you think…" Angela chortled. "I'm not blind, you idiot! The masseuse was blind!"

"Oh yeah."

Angela shook her head. "As if they would send a man to massage me."

"Yeah, but what about this scenario. I train to be a masseur, pretend to be blind and get a job in Sleeping Hands. I build up my reputation by massaging men, doing a great job, and then, when people hear about how good I am, I switch to women. After all, I'm blind, right?"

Angela laughed. "So you'd pretend to be blind so you could stare at naked women?"

"I'm not saying I would. Only that it's possible."

"Only in your warped imagination. Come on, drink up, I want to do some shopping before we leave tomorrow."

13

We spent our last morning in Pokhara wandering along the shore of the lake, browsing the shops and staring out over the water. An early morning mist had left tiny droplets of moisture on the leaves at the edge of the lake, and some cows were taking advantage of them with their long pink tongues.

Angela noticed a shop selling cupcakes and insisted we visit. She was obsessed with cupcakes, I'd discovered, and was even threatening to open a shop devoted to the things when we eventually moved back to the UK.

"You'll be disappointed," I said as we crossed towards the shop. "You always are."

Angela threw me a sideways look. "Not always. Remember that one in New England? And that one in Tokyo?"

"Okay: two out of two hundred. The odds are not good."

Angela went inside to buy a cake while I remained outside. A shoe shiner wandered past with his tools of the trade. He looked at my feet and walked on. Two minutes later, Angela came out with a cupcake. It had strawberry icing with a little dollop of cream. She took a tiny nibble (a morsel fit for a gnome), declared it tasty, and up to scratch. "I'll save the rest for the airport. I doubt there'll be a decent café inside the departure lounge. By the way, what time do we have to set off?"

I glanced at my watch. *Bloody hell!* Our Buddha Air flight back to Kathmandu left in less than an hour! Where had the time gone? "Now!" I exclaimed. "We should've set off half an hour ago!"

Angela wrapped her cake in the napkin it came with and set off at a manic walking pace with me hot on her heels. At one point, she deftly overtook a sleeping dog, and then a group of slow-moving locals. But then disaster struck – she lost her footing on a rough piece of kerb and collapsed into the road with a yelp and a bang, causing people to stop in their tracks, and me to almost trip over her. The hand with the cupcake was raised into the air, the napkin missing, and while I pondered whether to eat it, Angela jumped back on her feet, brushed herself down and dashed off again. With people staring agog, I rushed after her, wondering whether people thought I was some sort of assailant.

Five minutes later we stopped. "Oh my God," Angela said, panting breathlessly. We were off the main street, on the secluded lane that led to the New Pokhara Lodge. "How embarrassing!

Falling into the road like that. What must those people have thought? That's why I had to rush off."

"They've probably called the police by now. Deviant on the loose chasing women. Probably blind. Anyway, are you hurt?"

"No, thank God. At least I don't think so."

"What about the cake? I noticed you kept your hand in the air to protect it. Bugger saving your head or arm, as long as the cake survives."

Angela laughed. "The cake is okay. I can't believe my reflex action was to save it! I think you're right; I *am* obsessed with cupcakes."

Ten minutes later, we were in a taxi to the airport. Now that the adrenalin had worn off, Angela found out that she did have some pain, particularly in her lower back. But she was right about the airport café – it was threadbare on provisions, and especially meagre in the cake department. While I munched on a warm Bounty Bar, Angela ate the cupcake with relish. Not long after, we were aboard the Buddha Air turboprop bound for Kathmandu.

Top row: A man ponders his life aboard his boat; Angela sitting on the steps of the World Peace Pagoda
Middle row: Pokhara has lots of guest house; A cow licks the morning dew near Phewa Lake
Bottom row: I made it to the top to see the pink mountains; Street scene in downtown Pokhara

Chapter 6. Back to India

An indistinct Indian Ocean appeared beneath the left wingtip. The approach to Thiruvananthapuram Airport meant a low-level cloud run along the tropical beaches and palms that ran along the edge of the water. The orange sand was glowing as the blood-red sun began to set over the western horizon. We turned inland towards the runway and the pilot reduced speed, causing the aircraft to buffet in the turbulent hot skies of southern India. No one seemed concerned, though, least of all us. After so many flights, in far worse conditions than this, we were veterans of turbulence.

I looked down at the ever-nearing landscape. Colonial-style mansions and tin-roofed shacks came and went with dizzying speed. At one point, I spotted an aquamarine mosque, but in a flash it was gone, replaced by jungle. And then we touched down. Even before we had vacated the runway, ninety percent of the passengers had removed their seatbelts and were beginning to stand up in the aisle.

"Please remain seated," admonished a female member of the cabin crew. "The captain has not switched the fasten seatbelt signs off." She might as well have stopped the flow of water from an open tap. I'd once read that an irate pilot, faced with a similar situation, had braked heavily, causing all those standing to suddenly lunge forward and fall. Some had ended up with broken bones. Served them right, I thought. Over the intercom, the flight attendant told everyone to sit down again, but, as we trundled onto a taxiway, people were grabbing their baggage and already speaking into their phones. We had arrived in India again, the land that manners forgot.

2

Thiruvananthapuram Airport, or Trivandrum Airport as it was sometimes called – a name coined by British colonialists who thought the real name too difficult to pronounce – was pleasingly modern. Security was a breeze, and soon we were outside staring at the hundreds of people behind the barriers. All of them were studying us, and, as we made our way along the exit path, some were actually moving through the crowd with us.

"Taxi?" said one man in a string vest.

"You want taxi?" said another. He looked like he had three teeth.

"Where you go?" said a third man.

"First time in India?" said a fourth man, hopefully.

I shook my head to all requests, wondering where the official taxi booth was. The last thing we needed was to fall prey to these jackals. Angela spotted it first and we made a beeline towards it, negotiating the gauntlet of chancers and hopers trying to grab our suitcases to put them on trolleys. The man sitting behind the makeshift counter looked us up and down. "Where to?" he asked.

"Kovalam Beach," I stated, not wanting to say the name of our hotel just yet. If he knew where we were staying, the price would be much more, I was sure.

"Which hotel?"

I pretended I hadn't heard the question. "Kovalam Beach, please."

The man sighed. "Four hundred and seventy rupee."

I nodded. Less than a fiver for a thirty-minute journey. More than reasonable, I thought.

"Where about in Kovalam?" the taxi wallah asked.

"Vivanta by Taj," I said.

The wallah's eyes widened. "Vivanta?"

I nodded. "Four hundred and seventy rupees?"

The man nodded and lit a cigarette. He could have easily got three times that amount from us and knew it. He summoned a driver and told us to pay him the agreed amount upon arrival.

As expected, streets lights were of little concern to the town planners of Kerala. Compounding matters were the number of cars, motorbikes and auto-rickshaws without lights. Their only safety measure was their horns, which they used a lot. Our taxi had lights though, and they briefly illuminated bare-chested men wearing wrap-around sarongs. The road was decent and our driver skilful, and, less than half an hour later, we pulled up outside the hotel. From the din and dirt of an Indian backstreet, we were ushered into five-star opulence.

3

The next morning, we took in the tropical surrounds of our hotel. The sound of waves crashing against the shoreline, broken occasionally by a crow's squawk or the hoot of a beautifully plumaged blue bird, made us smile at the deliciousness of it all. Giant butterflies meandered and tumbled around flowers and thick green leaves, some of which were so immense that they were almost the size of trees,

"This is a world away from Delhi and Kathmandu," Angela announced, staring over the dense layer of palm trees that we could see from our balcony. Behind them, in the distance, a lagoon shimmered, and behind that was the blue expanse of ocean. "This is a tropical paradise."

After breakfast, we left the hotel and arrived into a hotbed of auto-rickshaw and taxi drivers. "You want to see lighthouse? You want to visit Kovalam Beach? Maybe ride to city?" The questions came thick and fast.

"Maybe later," I said, giving my stock response.

"Well, remember me," said one driver. "I'm driver number 704. My name is Naveen."

Angela and I walked along a palm-fringed pathway, flanked by the lagoon we had seen earlier. A couple of men, naked except for some baggy underpants, were in the middle of the water, standing at either end of a small wooden boat. One was bashing a stick into the water repeatedly, trying to scare the fish into their nets.

Suddenly, from out of nowhere, the largest bee I'd ever seen buzzed towards me. "Jesus!" I yelped, jolting my body to the side, causing a moment of panic to flash in Angela's eyes.

"What?" she screeched in alarm.

"A bee!" I bobbed my head as it took another dive, its stinger extended and primed. As it swooped past, I could hear its awful buzz. It sounded like a mini chainsaw. "A black and red one, with a massive stinger! Probably a killer bee!"

Angela spun around trying to spot the crazed insect. I did too, noticing that the men in the boat were still bashing the water, unaware that they were witnessing a deadly bee attack.

"*Where?*" she asked, her eyes flicking this way and that.

"I don't know!" I swung my head in all directions, but realised it must have gone. The last time I'd been so close to a bee was as a small child when one had stung me. It had been buzzing around my icecream, but, before my parents could do react, it had already stung me on the face. It was a horrific moment, made worse by the searing pain and the fact I dropped my cornet. And that was with a small British bumblebee, not this stripy monster. After scouting around for the bee for half a minute or so, we carried on walking along the path. "Angela, it was huge. Easily the biggest bee I've seen in my life."

And then I saw it again. It was coming in from my blind spot. I cried in alarm and danced in crazy circles. "It's back! It's going to sting me! It's going to bloody sting me!" But it didn't sting me and it disappeared again. My head flicked this way and that, trying to spot where the beast had gone. It was like a horror film.

Inexplicably, Angela started laughing. "You sound like a big girl. 'Ooh, the big bee is going to sting me! Ooh, it's a killer bee!'"

I ignored my wife. Perhaps my red T-shirt had angered the insect somehow. And what if it wasn't a bee? What if it was a wasp? They could sting repeatedly! While I pondered this, it attacked for a third time, this time diving towards the back of Angela's neck.

"Duck!" I yelled. "It's going for your jugular!"

Angela turned around, and her slipstream caused the bee to go wide. It righted itself and disappeared into a line of trees. Her eyes followed it, widening. "You were right; it *was* big. I take it all back."

We carried on, keeping a wary eye out for the red insect, until we passed a bewildered-looking hotel security guard. He eyed us suspiciously, clearly having seen the whole thing. To him, no doubt, we were either lunatics, new-age dancers or possibly high on hallucinogenic drugs.

4

The rolling waves of the Indian Ocean lapped against a thin strip of yellow sand. In the far distance was a small fishing boat, its single occupant barely visible as his vessel rose and dipped on the swell. On the beach were four young Western tourists, two men and two women. Instead of sunbathing or swimming, they were doing a strange routine of leaning against each other, standing up, legs spread apart. We left them to their yoga, or whatever it was, and wandered towards a set of small restaurants.

We sat down on the white plastic chairs and I perused the menu. It served mainly fish, which was fine by me. Curiously though, no beer was listed in the drinks section. When the waiter came over, we both ordered a fish curry and I asked whether he sold Kingfisher. He nodded almost imperceptibly. A few minutes later, my bottle of beer arrived wrapped up in newspaper. The waiter plonked a mug next to it and then poured me some beer. When he left, I looked around at the other tables – most had wrapped up bottles of beer on them.

"What's this about? I said to Angela, turning the bottle around in my hand. "Why the subterfuge? Is it illegal or something?"

A large older man in a white T-shirt who was sitting at the next table overheard me. He introduced himself as Joe, a Scot on holiday with his wife. She was sunbathing by the pool. "Aye, drinking in public is illegal in Kerala. And so is encouraging it. But I think the authorities turn a blind eye to places like this who serve a wee bit of beer to Westerners, as long as everyone's discreet – thus the paper wrapping."

"I see," I said, taking a sip from my mug. It didn't seem right to be drinking beer from a cup.

"But do you know the funny thing?" said Joe. "Kerala is the alcohol consumption capital of India. Their forced restriction has made things worse. It's like prohibition in America in the 1930s."

Just then, the waiter arrived with our fish curries and Joe excused himself, wishing us a happy stay in Kerala. We watched him go and then tasted one of the most delicious fish curries ever: huge chunks of white fish in a delectably spicy and tasty sauce. Thank God my taste buds were now in full working order. With the waves lapping only a few feet away, it was possibly the perfect place to have lunch.

5

We ambled towards the auto-rickshaw and taxi drivers loitering outside our hotel. All of them jumped up immediately. *Hello again! Taxi, sir? Auto-rickshaw, sir? See lighthouse? Beach? I take you there!*

We chose Naveen for the simple reason that he'd caught our eye first. He was a young man in his twenties with a great shock of black hair. The others took our decision well, regrouping at a nearby wall. We asked the auto-rickshaw driver to take us on a round trip to Kovalam Beach so we could see the lighthouse. "Plus," I said, "anywhere else you think would be good for photos."

Naveen nodded, and then wobbled his head until we agreed upon a price of 500 rupees for the one-hour trip. We climbed in the back and he cranked his tinny engine into life. Off we set, joining a busy main road designed for single-lane traffic. In Kerala, as in Delhi, lanes were meaningless. Road signs were useless too. Fly posters covered most of them.

"Did you see that shop sign?" Angela asked, as we hit the outskirts of town. She was grinning.

I shook my head.

"It was for a clinic. Two photos, side by side; both showing a man's lower legs and feet. The first photo was the 'before' shot. It showed his deformed feet splayed out at right angles, a bit like a duck."

I tried to picture the photo.

"The other photo was 'after' and showed some healthy, normal legs. So basically, if you go to their clinic, they can do that."

"And you doubt their claim?"

"What do you think?"

Music was blasting out from somewhere: high-pitched female singing that drowned out all other noise. She sounded like a banshee trainer. Every few seconds, the wailing built to a peak, and then, just as quickly, died away, only to be repeated further along the road. It took me a few minutes to work out that the din was coming from huge speakers on the side of the road. They were every few hundred metres, causing the endless wave of noise.

Naveen pulled over at the side of a particularly busy street. A line of parked trucks, minibuses and auto-rickshaws were blocking a road leading away from the main street; at first, I thought it was some sort of demonstration. I asked Naveen

"No demonstration," he said. "Temple blessing. Go see. I wait here, no problem."

Angela and I climbed out into what looked like a mini carnival.

6

People were everywhere. Some were hanging around by the side of road, simply chewing the fat, others were crowded around the empty parked vehicles, most of which, we now noticed, were covered in colourful garlands. One man was standing next to a brightly-painted pink and yellow bus emblazoned with the name: Holy Mutha. Another man was blessing his bus by sprinkling water over it. Across the front grille, someone had placed a necklace of flowers. I guessed it was some sort of Hindu festival.

At the bottom of some steps was a small temple covered in the most preposterous paint scheme ever. A riot of pinks, yellows, greens and yellows dazzled our eyes. In front of it, women sat on the floor with trays of fish, nuts and fruit. Others sat at roadside stoves made from bricks, cooking foil-wrapped fish for passing pilgrims.

I was thirsty, and so we stepped over the makeshift stoves towards a small open-fronted shop. A beaming man bounded out as soon as he spied us and regarded us expectantly. We entered his shop and the man followed, looking like he had won the lottery. I looked in the fridge and saw what I wanted. "Two diet cokes, please," I said.

"Only two, sir. How about three?"

I shook my head. "Just two, please."

The man nodded and retrieved the bottles, and motioned that I should join him at the counter. Behind it were four young women in colourful saris. All of them looked at me, and I smiled, but this caused one of them to burst out laughing. I turned to Angela but she hadn't noticed. I looked back at the women and now one of them was pointing at me. They all looked on the verge of hilarious laughter, and I wondered what was wrong. The man ignored his harem and handed me the cola bottles. "Sixty rupees, sir. But are you sure you do not want anything else?" He leaned in close. "Like maybe...you know...?"

He let the statement hang in the air. The women were still staring and giggling, chattering away among themselves, and I regarded the shopkeeper. What did he mean by that? What was he trying to say? With Angela busy looking at a shelf stocked with creams and ointments, I could only conclude that he was trying to flog me the local variety of Viagra. It would probably make me go blind. I shook my head. "No thanks."

"Well, how about something to help you sleep at night, sir?" The man was not about to give up without a fight. "Have you been sleeping well recently?"

"All I want are the drinks."

The man nodded. "What about water. So hot outside. Water very cheap!"

"No thanks. But I will have a packet of *Masala Munch*." The packet of crisps had caught my eye due to its snazzy title.

The man reluctantly took my hundred-rupee note and passed it to one of the women. Transaction complete, we headed outside to the auto-rickshaw. It was time to go to the beach. The Masala Munch turned out to be horrible.

7

Kovalam Beach was a wide strip of sand lined with sun loungers, gift shops, fish restaurants and men trying to hawk little wooden elephants and tacky leaf paintings. One establishment claimed it offered foot massages. Fair enough, but the accompanying photograph showed a near naked man standing on someone's back. The focus was on the first man's hairy feet.

The strip was busy with tourists, and the ratio compared to locals was about even. A thin, bare-chested Western man wearing baggy tie-dyed pants was walking towards us. He was in his fifties, and with his dreadlocked hair, matted beard and moustache (worn in the style favoured by Gurus) he looked *wrong*.

"He's been here too long," I said when he'd passed. "He probably came in the seventies and stayed put. He'll have a cannabis farm in the hills."

The lighthouse looked impressive. It was a tall red and white striped tower, which at night cast a powerful and revolving beam into the dark sky. The guidebook said it was possible to climb it, but, as far as we could tell, the gate was locked. Instead we returned to the tuk-tuk.

Our next stop was a bright, lime-green mosque, looking like it had been constructed from candy. A goat was scavenging on the measly offerings nearby, and it eyed us balefully as we climbed out of the auto-rickshaw.

Naveen led us up some steps at the side of the mosque where we found a locked door. It appeared that we would not be going inside. Instead, Naveen pointed out a fishing village across the bay called Vizhinjam. Scores of small, blue and red striped fishing boats were sloshing about in the shallows or resting on the beach. Fishing was over for the day, and the only activity was a few repair jobs: a couple of men fixing nets and another looking at the inner workings of his outboard motor. Behind the boats was a small village, and then an immense jungle of lofty palms. The most striking feature in the village was a huge white tower attached to a tall white building. I thought it was a Hindu temple, but Naveen told us it was called Saint Mary's Church.

"So Christians, Hindus and Muslims live together in the same place?" asked Angela.

Naveen nodded. "In same village but own area. In 1995, very bad thing happen in Vizhinjam. Big riot. Two people die. Christian and Muslim fishermen had big fight. They smash each other's huts and boats. Fire everywhere. Two Muslim men killed with poles. Riot only stop when police come with guns."

We drove into Vizhinjam itself, traversing its busy backstreets filled with hardware stores, fried food shacks and men sitting about in doorways. At the end of a thin, sand-strewn street we came to a small square dominated by the striking white church we'd seen earlier. Six storeys high, the tapering place of worship was topped with a cross and a golden (and distinctly Indian) version of the Virgin Mary and Jesus. A young woman wearing a red and green sari emerged from the doors and disappeared into a nearby side street.

Back outside the Vivanta, we paid Naveen his fare (and a little extra) and promised we would look out for him again.

"Thank you," he said, grinning, revealing some impossibly white teeth that the dentists of Kathmandu would kill for, "but maybe give other drivers chance next time. We all wait outside your hotel. It is the fair way to do things."

8

Journeying on a houseboat is a major tourist activity in Kerala. It involves boarding a grand, fully equipped wooden barge, complete with a private captain and chef, and travelling sedately along the palm-fringed backwaters of Kerala for a few days of peace and quiet. With only a short time in Kerala, we didn't have time for that and so asked a small travel agent near the hotel about the possibility of doing a day trip along the backwaters.

"Of course, sir," said the keen-eyed man behind the counter, "we have boat trips to suit any wish or desire."

We sat down and the man told us he could arrange a trip the next day. He pointed out the range of boats available on a large poster behind him, telling us the differences between them. We liked the sound of a covered boat for a three-hour round trip.

"Very good choice, sir. Our driver will pick you up from your hotel for private boat trip around backwaters. Very relaxing. You will see many wild creatures and also see floating village. Then maybe have some lunch and visit an island. Does that sound acceptable?"

I looked at Angela. She was nodding.

"How much?" I asked.

The man paused, as if considering how much he could ask for without overdoing it. It was sometimes a fine line. "Five thousand rupees," he said, almost fifty quid.

I shook my head and laughed. "No, too much."

"But your trip is inside a covered boat made from bamboo! And tour is only for two people. Private backwater trips very expensive, you know. But, okay, for you, I drop price to four thousand if you pay a deposit today."

I could tell Angela was itching to seal the deal, and so I handed over a thousand rupees. In return, the man gave us a receipt. "Driver will pick you up at 10am sharp, sir."

9

That evening we caught another auto-rickshaw to Kovalam Beach. With the sun going down over the ocean, men wearing luminous red devil horns tried to attract our attention, as did men playing small drums. Along the strip, the restaurants were in full swing, with fresh fish laid out for inspection. One featured a swordfish; its sharp protrusion had a red tomato on the end.

After something to eat, we entered a shop so I could purchase a bottle opener. Earlier that day, I'd bought two bottles of Kingfisher Beer from a government-approved liquor store, the only place to buy alcohol legally in Kerala. Two men had been working behind the wire-mesh fronted store: one to take my order, deal with the money and hand me a slip of paper, the other to read my slip of paper, go to the fridge and hand me my bottles in a bag. All done without a single word of conversation. Why it needed two men to do this job was anyone's guess, but it did leave me with the problem of how to open them.

As Angela made a beeline for some ornaments, I milled around in the shop, trying to find the most likely place for a bottle opener to reside. I headed towards some cooking utensils, and as I did so, the proprietor approached.

"Looking for something in particular, sir?" he asked. His voice was unnaturally high-pitched, and, for a moment, I thought it was a woman.

"Yes: a bottle opener."

He wobbled his head. "I beg your pardon, sir?"

"A bottle opener." I mimed opening a bottle.

"Ah, we do not sell, I'm afraid."

"I see. No problem." I was about to find Angela when the man leaned in close to me, the second shopkeeper to do so in as many days. "Sir, maybe you want to look further at my stock? Perhaps there are more important things to open than…a bottle." He was nodding earnestly.

I thanked the man, but went off to find Angela anyway. Soon after, we departed his strange store of magic and intrigue.

10

As promised, a driver picked us up promptly at 10am. When we hit the main road, I noticed the vehicles covered in flowers were gone, as was the constant wailing from the speakers. A man carrying an oversized bundle on his back was causing a jam up ahead though. It didn't help that someone had dumped half a ton of rubble by the side of the road, which meant he had to veer into the road to get around it, meaning we all had to swerve around him.

Occasionally we passed plush homes belonging to the rich of Kerala. Painted in blues, yellows, purples and pinks, these large, almost colonial-style houses featured sweeping verandas, flat-topped roofs, air-conditioning units and satellite dishes. Tropical vegetation and shacks surrounded them.

Twenty minutes later, our car turned along a dirt track that bumped us over uneven ground until we ended up by a riverbank. A collection of small boats were tethered in the water, and a shack that looked like it might be a taxi stand stood nearby. A few men were sitting near it on white plastic chairs. Kerala seemed to have an abundance of white plastic chairs. Our driver led us to the boats where a young man was waiting. He was called Harsha, a wiry individual who looked about sixteen. We were soon on our way.

An endless expanse of coconut trees and jungle flanked both sides of the river. White, long-necked birds stood motionless in the shallows at the edge, peering into the water. Angela pointed out a dazzlingly beautiful blue and white kingfisher darting around some reeds, its plumage shimmering like jewellery. Above the river circled a vast array of sea eagles: most riding the thermals. Every so often, one would swoop in to the river.

"Snake bird," said Harsha, pointing. In the water was a black bird with an elongated neck. It was sitting on a wooden stump jutting out of the water, and I had to admit that, because of its neck, it did resemble a snake. When we got too close, it jumped from its perch and dived into the river, disappearing from sight.

We powered onward through the backwaters of Kerala. Apart from the occasional boat of life-jacketed sightseers, we had the streams to ourselves. I took a photo of Angela enjoying the trip, and she took one of the large wet patch on my shorts. It was from a coconut we'd bought earlier. When the man in the wooden boat had passed it to me, it slipped and emptied half its contents over my lap. It turned out to be quite refreshing.

We came to an opening in the jungle. The clearing led to a few shacks, and in front of them, a trio of goats munched on the undergrowth. The residents of the shacks were in the water in front of the goats, washing themselves – about six people in total. We waved, but none returned the gesture.

Around the next bend, I caught sight of a monkey. It was on all fours, making its way through the tangle of mangrove and forest. I nudged Angela and pointed.

"Where?" she said, straining to see.

"There. Just behind that line of trees. It's low down, walking along."

Angela peered into along the riverbank. "I can't see it."

I sighed. "Look! There, you blind bat."

"Where?"

The monkey was disappearing into the thick jungle. I could barely see it now and knew it would be pointless trying to get my wife to see it. "It's gone now. Forget it."

The river widened into a larger expanse of water. A long sandbank was on one side, and a few floating restaurants on the other. Harsha seemed to be heading towards one. I leaned in towards Angela. "Why are we going there?" I whispered. "We've only just had breakfast."

Angela looked at her watch. We'd been aboard the boat for little more than half an hour. Was that it? Tour over by eleven o' clock? If it was, then it was a rubbish tour of Kerala's backwaters, and I would have to say something. We pulled up at the restaurant's small jetty, where a smiling man appeared. Behind him, up on the main deck, a couple of bored-looking waiters were hanging around. "Good day, sir," said Mr Smiley. "Welcome to my floating restaurant."

I said hello and then turned back to Harsha. "We're not hungry," I told him. "We've only just had breakfast."

"No problem, sir. Just order food now. We come back later."

"So we're not stopping here now?"

"No, sir. Tour much more! We still have beautiful beach near Arabian Sea to visit. Then we see floating village and amazing island. Only order food for later."

I turned back to the proprietor who thrust a couple of menus at us. The prices were not extortionate but we had paid for a three-hour tour of the backwater of Kerala, and sitting in a restaurant for part of that did not seem fair. "Look," I whispered to Angela, "we might be hungry in an hour or so. I reckon we order from this menu and be done with it. It sounds like we've got lots more to see." Angela flicked over a page. The owner was waiting patiently, a grin etched on his face.

"Very good fish," he offered, "and delectable crab!"

We made our order and the man disappeared, yelling something to his waiting minions. As for us, we were already setting off towards the sandbank I'd noticed earlier.

11

"This can't be the beach he was talking about, can it?" I said. Angela didn't reply. We were standing about three feet above the waves on a narrow and treeless sandbank. In front of us was an endless expanse of ocean, with rolling and crashing surf tickling the lower reaches of the sand. It was okay as far as beaches went, but if we'd wanted to sit by the ocean, there were much nicer beaches by the hotel.

It had taken Harsha about three minutes to cross from the floating restaurant to his so-called amazing beach near the Arabian Sea. After he'd dropped us off, he told us he would return after thirty minutes so we could continue with the tour. Before we could say anything, he was starting his motor and turning around. He had marooned us.

"This is a poor tour of the backwaters," Angela said, bending down to study a coconut shell. It looked like a monkey's face. "A waste of money."

Further along the sandbank, four Western tourists were sunbathing. They didn't seem overly concerned about being abandoned on a thin strip of sand. "Maybe it's us," I said. "Maybe we're too fussy?" Angela was staring at a group of fishing boats huddled together out on the surf.

"No," she said sharply. "We booked this tour with the promise of a three-hour boat ride. How long have we had so far? Thirty minutes, forty at most? It's a con. And that floating village he was talking about: I hope it's not that." She pointed at a collection of twenty or so thatched wooden huts on stilts. But they didn't look ramshackle or rustic in any way. The air conditioning units, and wooden balconies overlooking the river made me think they were holiday rentals for rich tourists. They certainly were not part of a local backwater village.

I pointed to an outcrop just a little further along from the holiday homes. "And that will be the tropical island."

Angela smirked. "It won't be."

I turned to look at the ocean. There was something relaxing about staring at a large expanse of water, and this was no different. We found a dry spot on the sand and sat down. In the end, it wasn't a bad way to spend half an hour.

12

Lunch turned out to be quite tasty. It was a little disconcerting to be the only people eating in the restaurant, but the view was nice and the breeze refreshing. Afterwards, we returned to the boat with Harsha for the second half of the boat trip. First stop was the floating village.

Angela was correct. The floating village *was* the series of high-end holiday villas on the water's edge we'd seen from the sandbank. In one of them, an elderly Western man was sitting on a balcony reading a book.

My joke about the island being the rocky outcrop also turned out to be true. And what made it worse was that it wasn't actually an island: a litter-infested causeway connected it to the mainland. Nevertheless, we powered towards it and Harsha switched off his raspy motor. We duly clambered out of the boat, climbed some steps and stood at eye-level next to a large silver statue of Mary and Jesus. Perhaps sensing that we were not overawed by his boat tour, Harsha offered to take a series of photos of us. That done, we climbed back down, vaulted across the litter and returned to the boat.

"We go back now," Harsha muttered as he took up station at the back. "Tour finish."

I nodded resignedly. What a waste of money. Forty pounds for a forty minutes boat tour. They had seen us coming. Still, we had seen some of the backwaters, and had seen a tiny fragment of village life in rural Kerala. Plus, the birds had been good.

"This tour," Angel whispered, "should be done under the Trade Descriptions Act."

"Yeah," I whispered back. "Describing those holiday homes as a floating village? What a joke! It's like telling visitors to England that they are going to drive past a village on wheels. Then they see a caravan park. Ridiculous."

"Well, it's done now so we can stop moaning."

13

That evening, as the sun began to set, we went for a meal at the same small ocean-side restaurant just along from our hotel. The fish curry was again delicious, the newspaper-wrapped bottle of beer less so. Part of the newspaper had the most bizarre crossword known to man. One across read: *Flummox, kidnap monarch in silence and place head there.*

"How many letters?" Angela asked.

"Does it matter? Six."

Angela thought for a moment and then gave up so I read 20 down. "Four letters. *German approval overturned to get short hacker programming web development techniques.*"

Angela laughed. "You're making it up."

"I'm not. See for yourself." I spun the bottle around.

I ate another mouthful of my curry. It really was the tastiest spiced fish I'd ever had. To my left, I could hear the crash of waves as they pounded against a small headland. Lines of tropical palms were swaying in the light ocean breeze. It was an idyllic spot to watch the sunset from.

"Remember that growth on my knee I showed you in Pokhara?" I said.

Angela pulled a pained expression. "How could I forget?"

"Well, it's worse now. It looks like a fish eye. It's got—"

"Shut up! Don't tell me. You're disgusting. Horrible!"

I looked at the strange thing. It really did look like a fish eye, especially with the black dot in the middle of the milky white circle. And Angela was right: it *was* disgusting, and it worried me too. What if something had bitten me, or what if some critter had laid its eggs inside me? Maybe it would hatch in the night, and then forage its way out from under my skin, *Alien*-like. It didn't bear thinking about, and so I pressed it, still finding it firm to the touch. At least it didn't hurt.

"Stop fiddling with it," hissed Angela. "Leave it alone. You're ruining a perfectly good evening."

"Should I see a doctor, do you think?"

Angela grimaced. "I don't know. But it's not normal, is it? I mean, to have a fish eye growing out of your knee."

I looked at my growth and thought I saw it blink.

14

The next morning was our final day in India and I was reading a couple of English-language newspapers over breakfast. *The Hindu* contained not one but six separate articles about the Indian railway system. New fares, slipshod interim rail budgets and the dismal state of some toilets aboard trains took up huge amounts of valuable column inches. Another article inside the newspaper repeated what all the others had stated. The newspaper was obsessed with trains.

The New Indian Express, whose name sounded like a train, led with a story about locomotion too. In the lead article, the reporter described how a decade of neglect would befall India's rail system if the new rail budget went ahead. I bypassed the story and read about an elderly woman who had left her home in the middle of the night, stumbled across an open well and fallen in. Her dead body was discovered two days later.

Brutal Police Attack on Senior Citizen was another headline. During a protest against the widening of a road in Kerala, some pensioners had become agitated. When the police arrived, the pensioners refused to back down, and, in an attempt to subdue one of the ring leaders, an officer had grabbed the senior citizen's genitals and pulled him to his jeep. Someone had taken a photo. The grainy snap showed an old man, with a walking stick, bent double, while a police officer tugged at his trousers. It was hard to make out the detail, and, for all I knew, the officer could've been pulling the man by his belt, which was exactly what the policeman had claimed. The article closed by stating a probe was under way.

I closed the paper and took a sip of my coffee. It was lukewarm. Angela's expression wasn't. "Fifteen minutes you've been reading that paper. Over the breakfast table. I might as well have not been here."

"You should've said something."

Angela's glare softened. "You were engrossed. What was so interesting?"

"Trains and pensioner abuse. Oh, and a story about an old lady who fell down a well and died."

"That's terrible." Angela turned her gaze out over the swimming pool and the jungle beyond. A bright-red bird was skimming between coconut palms. By the pool, a crow landed and took a sneaky sip.

"Come on," I said, "time to see the big city."

15

Thiruvananthapuram dates back thousands of years. King Solomon reportedly visited in 1036BC when it was a major trading point for the sale and movement of spices and ivory. By the middle ages, Thiruvananthapuram became a city of murder and intrigue, as various Mughals and royal families fought over power. Today, it is home to three-quarters of a million people and is one of the major IT hubs in India.

The thirty-minute journey took us past the usual sights of urban India – piles of rubbish, auto-rickshaw repair shops, fruit stands and fires.

Many Indian roads had flames dancing at their edges, with crows and white egrets pecking at the whitening embers of coconut shells and other garbage. Limping dogs and stick-thin men hobbled in the dust by the verge. The air smelled of fumes and smoke. But the traffic was always moving. Any road blockage was a mere moment of angry beeping and never a calamity. Even a man pushing what amounted to a dining table on wheels, full to the brim with watermelons, couldn't stop the flow of traffic.

Thiruvananthapuram was a different matter. Traffic lights could stop vehicles in their tracks, and they did with wanton abandon. Lines of cars, lorries and buses with open-air windows sat stationary in the stifling air. And, when the lights turned to green, woe betide any drivers who failed to set off in time; the full force of a hundred angry horns beeping simultaneously would jolt them into quick motion. But even the big city traffic lights could not halt a fleet-footed cow running down the middle of one street. Blithely unaware of the mayhem it had created, the beast stopped outside a shop and loitered, swished its tail around for a moment and then sat down. The traffic moved again en masse.

16

Our first stop was a gigantic Hindu Temple dedicated to Lord Vishnu. The auto-rickshaw driver dropped us off and told us to take as much time as we wanted. "I wait all day if you want."

The Sree Padmanabhaswamy Temple rose over the grime of the city like a carved skyscraper. Its tall, tapering tower, full of statues and decorations, looked as if master craftsmen had chiselled it from ivory. Men wearing orange belts and *dhoti*, white wraparound sheets covering from the waist to the ankles, were wandering up and down the steps near the entrance of the temple. They were Hindus, and their attire was needed in order for them to enter the place of worship.

Angela and I walked to the steps and milled around at the bottom, wondering what to do. A small man at the top was waving, gesturing that we should go up. A brown-uniformed policeman with a hefty assault rifle was standing next to him. He looked bored and, after regarding us for a few seconds, looked away. I pointed my shorts out to the waving man, sure that they would bar entry to the temple, but he continued to wave us up. We both climbed the steps to meet him.

The first thing that struck me was the man's size. He was about as tall as an eleven-year-old boy. The second thing was his teeth – or rather tooth, singular, because that's all he had. But at least it was a big shiny white one.

"My name Rajeev," he said, forcing a smile with his inadequate mouth. "You no allow in temple, but I show you other side. Come." His accent was strong and I could hardly understand him. The bored policeman stared at us, but said nothing as we passed.

Rajeev took us past the main entrance and started describing some features of the temple but I caught very little of what he said, and, judging by her expression, neither did Angela. Instead, we resorted to nodding our heads at suitable times in his monologue, occasionally saying, *I see*. One thing I did catch was the age of the temple.

"Five thousand years old?" I said, astonished. "Are you sure?" That would make it older than the Great Pyramids of Giza.

"Yes! Five thousand years old! I tell no lie!"

Later I would find out it was only about 250 years old.

Rajeev led us around a corner to another entrance, this one much smaller. At first, I thought he was going to take us in, but when a guard stuck his arm out, blocking my path, I knew this wasn't going to happen.

"Only Hindu go in," said Rajeev. "But look, yes please!"

Rajeev spoke to the guard, who gave us the once over and then moved so we could peer inside. Beyond the entrance was a dark corridor full of women selling trinkets. Behind them was an elephant draped in flowers.

"Come," Rajeev said. "I show statue." He led us along a side lane along the northern edge of the temple where he stopped to point out a statue high above our heads. He then rambled on about it for a full five minutes. I caught about one percent of what he'd said. Angela was looking at her watch, and, when Rajeev paused for breath, we thanked him but said we had to go.

Back at the main entrance near the steps, Rajeev suddenly became quiet and shuffled from foot to foot. And that's when I noticed one of his feet was huge. He looked like he was suffering from elephantitis. I fished out a hundred rupee note from my wallet and handed it to him. He took it and nodded.

17

The streets of Thiruvananthapuram were busy with shoppers, hawkers, traffic and noise. The ladies of India were browsing the cloth stalls in large groups, while their menfolk whipped up sales in the chat houses and bakeries. We passed a stall selling huge bundles of grapes at 40 rupees for half a kilogram, and then a gaudy shop selling balloons and green blow-up animals: Pankaj Fancy, the shop's name proudly boasted. All along the street, tiny shops that sold knick-knacks and textiles had given themselves grand names: the Textile Palace, Fancy Emporium and Kingdom of Cloth. We walked further along and spied two men huddled under a sheet, fixing umbrellas. I'd never seen such a thing in my life, and neither had Angela. In the UK, if an umbrella was damaged, the owner would simply throw it away and buy a new one. Not so in Thiruvananthapuram. Recycling such as this had been going on for centuries in India.

We met up with our auto-rickshaw driver. In a job where the bread and butter of his day was picking up locals for 30 or 40 rupees a ride, bagging a couple of tourists was the cream. "Where you want to go next, sir?" he asked, beaming.

"The zoo, please."

"Zoo?"

"Yes. With the animals." I growled like a lion for good effect. Angela rolled her eyes but it did the trick.

"Ah, yes, sir. Animals. Very good!"

He turned the key, gunned his pedal and off we trundled along the main drag of the city, Mahatma Gandhi Road, or MG Road as it was locally known. Proud colonial-era buildings and fine churches vied for position among shacks selling building materials. A huge stationery shop boasted that it was Kerala's largest. We alighted at the far end of the road, and the driver told us to take our time. "Animals, that way," he said. "I wait here."

We headed for the zoo.

18

Neither Angela nor I were fans of zoos, and yet in Thiruvananthapuram we were about to visit our second of our trip. But there was a particular reason why we wanted to: Thiruvananthapuram Zoo happened to be the inspiration behind the book *Life of Pi*.

Canadian-born author Yann Martel spent some time in Thiruvananthapuram Zoo in 1996, studying the animals, learning about their behaviour and that of visitors too, collecting details and colour to add to his story. His interest in one tiger in particular provided him with the seed for his Man Booker prize-winning novel. Both Angela and I had loved the film, and wanted to see where a little bit of the story had hatched.

Thiruvananthapuram Zoo was one of India's first. Founded in 1857, it wowed local people with its jungle creatures and exotic fauna. For the first time, people could see a tiger up close, or a leopard, and live to tell the tale. With each wild animal contained within sturdy metal cages, people flocked in their thousands to gawp, point and sometimes throw things. Little has changed with regard to human behaviour since those early days, but the enclosures have grown in size, and the ground beneath most of the animals is more akin to their natural habitats as opposed to bare concrete.

At the entrance gate, the man sitting at a table asked us whether we were carrying any water.

"Why," I asked, "is there a problem if we are?" It seemed an unusual thing to ask.

The man smiled. "No problem, sir." He explained that the zoo had a problem with water bottles. When visitors finished with them, he explained, they sometimes threw the empty bottles at the animals or else littered them on the ground. "So now we ask for a deposit. Then we put sticker on bottle. When you come back and show the sticker, I give deposit money back."

I handed the man a few crumpled rupees and the man duly stuck a sticker on our bottle. He then wrote the sticker number down in a ledger and recorded the amount of money we'd given. We thanked him and entered the zoo.

"What a great idea," said Angela as we ambled towards the enclosures. "They should do that everywhere."

We spied a white-haired monkey sitting on a rock. It resembled Peter Stringfellow, the London playboy. It wasn't doing much, so we walked over to a snake house that contained a king cobra. Because it was one of the deadliest animals on the planet, the 12-foot black snake could only be viewed from the outside, through some dirty window panes. As a further safety precaution, a barrier encircled the enclosure, stopping anyone from getting too close. We peered through the murky glass and saw that the serpent was slumbering. Above it was an open window. Someone had left a pair of ladders there.

"Can snakes climb things?" I asked Angela. I pointed at the open window.

"I would think so."

"So if that thing wakes up and decides to climb to the window, then we've had it. All it's got to do is slither down the ladders and it's free."

We carried on with our walk around the zoo, passing birds of prey cooped up inside small curved cages, and fruit bats hanging from tall tree branches, their only movement the occasional unfurling of their pterodactyl-like wings. We stared at hippos and rhinos lounging about in the sun, and a frisky antelope trying to mount any female he could catch. And then we came to the big cats. Two tigers, a pair of lions and a single jaguar were contained inside small individual enclosures tucked away behind thick metal bars. They looked like prisoners. Unlike what we'd hoped for, the beautiful creatures were living on bare concrete. Their great size, coupled with their tiny cages, made them seem like giants. All of them were asleep.

"This is horrible," whispered Angela, as we stared into the cage of a nine-year-old tiger, "and precisely why I don't like zoos. I can't believe any author would get inspiration from *this*."

The silence was shattered by the arrival of a group of unsupervised schoolchildren. They were aged about thirteen and all of them were laughing and joking, creating a hullabaloo as they came along. One boy started growling at one of the sleeping tigers, and another started shouting at a lion. None of the cats moved and so a few more children joined in with the racket. Thankfully it didn't have any effect on the animals, not even when one of the boys started banging his water bottle on the bars. Angela and I were sufficiently disgusted that we decided to leave the zoo. We found our auto-rickshaw and climbed into the vehicle in a sombre mood.

19

We watched the sunset from our favourite table overlooking the ocean. My fish curry was again delicious, as was Angela's spiced fish meal. A middle-aged Russian-looking couple was sitting at the next table to us. For the entire duration of their meal, they didn't say one word to each other. Instead, they sat bent low, close to their bowls, shovelling food like there was no tomorrow. Angela and I were quick eaters, but the Russians were in another league. After a slurp from his mug of Kingfisher, the man finished, and, two seconds later, so did his wife. A few moments later, they called the waiter over and asked for the bill. They quickly paid it and were off. It was a master class in speed eating.

The sky was turning from red to maroon, and we were both gazing at a fishing boat sloshing about in the distance. It was anchored for the night and was now the roost for a flock of seabirds.

"Here's to India," I said, raising my mug of beer. Angela picked up her mug of wine and we clinked them together.

"And here's to Sri Lanka," she said. Country number four was just over the horizon.

Top row: Looking along Kovalam beach to the lighthouse; A mosque near the village of Vizhinjam
Middle row: A coconut shell Angela found on a beach near the Arabian Sea; Angela and me enjoying our tour of the backwaters
Bottom row: The prow of our boat as we toured the backwaters of Kerala; Street scene in Kerala

Chapter 7. Colombo and the Elephant Festival

When we boarded our Sri Lankan Airlines flight to Colombo, there was a man sitting in my seat. He was a Sri Lankan gent and looked nonplussed when I pointed out his error. I showed him my boarding card but he looked at it blankly. He wasn't the only one in the wrong seat. Scores of people had simply sat where they liked with no care for their assigned places. In the end, a courteous cabin crewmember sorted things out with a patience I would never have possessed. But even when the seats had been sorted, there was still work for her to do.

"You need to put your seatbelt on, sir," she said to the Sri Lankan man sitting in the row behind us.

No response.

"You need to put your seatbelt on for take-off, sir."

"I no want to."

"Well, in that case, you'll have to leave the aircraft."

A few seconds later, it clicked into place. Normal service resumed, and, an hour after leaving the runway in India, we touched down in Sri Lanka on what promised to be a warm, tropical day.

2

Sri Lanka was another feast of colour. Fruit and vegetable hawkers plied the area by the side of the airport road; dogs lazed in and among them while ornately coloured trucks puffed out blasts of smoke as they blindly pulled into moving traffic. We passed small Buddhist shrines surrounded by flowers, and plenty of women carrying pots on their head. Sri Lanka was cut from the same piece of cloth as India.

The Galle Face Hotel is an institution in Sri Lanka. Built in 1864, its literature proudly boasts it is the oldest hotel east of the Suez. Located on the coast, it overlooks the Indian Ocean, and seems exquisitely colonial with its verandas, sea front patios and lines of palm trees. There was even a ninety-two year old man called K. Chattu Kuttan sitting by the entrance, ushering people into the grand lobby. He waved as we passed him, looking resplendent in his white uniform (adorned with gold trim and a chest full of medals), white hair and white handlebar moustache.

Kuttan first started working at the hotel in 1942 after taking the ferry across from his homeland in Kerala. He started his employment as a waiter, and was only promoted to doorman in the 1990s. He was, reportedly, the oldest bellboy in the world, and, as such, had become the face of the Galle Face Hotel.

After unpacking a few things, we decided to see what Colombo had to offer, and found ourselves on a side street full of auto-rickshaws (now known as tuk-tuks). Ahead of us was a long promenade following the ocean, with a stupendously tall pole holding a colourful Sri Lankan flag at the top. A few tuk-tuk drivers tried to gain our attention, but we waved them off as we made our way to the roundabout on the main road.

"So far, so good," I said as we ambled along. It was hot, but not overbearingly so yet. And, though Colombo did not have the wow factor of Kerala, it didn't look too shabby. In fact, it looked quite nice, in a run-down sort of way.

"Yeah," agreed my wife, "so far, so good."

3

"It is too warm," a local man said as he passed us. Angela and I were strolling along, minding our own business. He was a small gent with a leathery but friendly face. He looked about forty.

Neither of us replied, but the man slowed nonetheless and then stopped. "You staying at Galle Face?" he asked.

Angela nodded.

"I knew so! I see you today. I work as gardener in hotel. I see you arrive."

I nodded but still said nothing. The amount of times strangers had approached us, who had then turned out to be hustlers, touts or beggars, was countless and it made us naturally cautious. We walked past the man but he decided to join us, asking about where we were from, whether it was our first time in Sri Lanka and how long we were staying in Colombo. They were standard questions for a hustler but equally they were standard questions from an inquisitive stranger too.

"Galle Face very nice hotel," he said, seemingly satisfied with the one-word answers we'd given him so far. "Give me lots of work. And that is where I must go now. So, enjoy your stay in Colombo. Goodbye." As he veered away in the general direction of the Galle Face, I raised my eyebrows at Angela. "I thought he was going to ask for money or something."

"Me too."

Just then, the gardener stopped and turned around. "If you are heading to the elephant festival, you must hurry."

"Elephant festival?" asked Angela.

The man nodded. "Yes. I thought you knew. Elephant festival is along this street, but very far. That is why I tell you to hurry. I think it end quite soon."

I told him we didn't know anything about the elephant festival.

The man's eyes widened. "Really? You must go! Over one hundred elephants, all of them parading!"

We wondered what to do. If there was an elephant parade along this road somewhere, then that was something we ought to see. But we didn't know anything about it – we didn't even have a guidebook yet. And what if the man was lying? Perhaps sensing our hesitation, the gardener addressed us again. "Just walk along this street and you will see the elephants. You will take many good photos! Goodbye." He started to walk away again, heading for some shade under a line of trees.

Angela and I stood on the side of the street, pondering our options. We'd only planned to do a quick walk around the vicinity of the hotel, but with the prospect of a hundred elephants – doing a parade, no less – the game had changed. "Let's just walk down the road and see what's down there," I said.

Angela looked along the road and then at the gardener. He was almost out of sight. "Okay. Let's do it."

We set off walking but a loud whistle made us pause. It was the gardener again. He was walking towards us, still smiling. "Look, may I offer you some help?" he said when he'd caught up. "If you want to see elephants, then maybe get tuk-tuk. I think it is too far to walk and not enough time."

It sounded like fair advice.

"But only get government tuk-tuk," the man warned, "others will rip you off. I will show you how to spot a government tuk-tuk so you will know." The man scanned some of the passing vehicles and shook his head. "No good. They will rip you off. That one too is not good. Look at colour – private vehicle. Hang on, there is one." He pointed to one parked a little way up the street. "Wait though, maybe he is government…I check for you." He walked over to the red tuk-tuk and spoke to the driver. He returned to us. "He okay. Government tuk-tuk. No problem with him. I have explained to driver where you want to go."

We thanked the gardener, who had really gone out of his way to assist us, and climbed into the back of the red tuk-tuk. After agreeing on a price of 500 rupees (£2.30) to take us to the elephant parade and back, we set off. Our gardener friend was already crossing the road towards the hotel.

4

Within a few minutes, we stopped at a police roadblock. An armed guard looked at the driver's ID and then studied us in the back. He nodded at the driver, returned his ID and allowed us to move on.

"No worry about police," shouted the driver over the rush of air percolating through the open-sided vehicle. "Normal for Sri Lanka."

Well, at least the driver's credentials had checked out, I thought, as we sped along the street. After passing a collection of fruit stands, we turned onto a side street and slowed down. There was a temple ahead of us on the right-hand side. Angela and I strained our necks to see the elephants. There weren't any.

"Elephant temple," said the tuk-tuk driver, pulling over to the side of the road and switching his engine off. "Come, I take you inside."

We followed the man into a courtyard full of statues, mainly of lions and multi-armed gods. Bizarrely, there was also a vintage Mercedes car parked at one end, but whether it was on display was anyone's guess. A man in a stall handed Angela a wraparound sarong in return for a few rupees and then we entered the temple. The main room contained a large orange Buddha that wasn't particularly inspiring and so we turned around to go. We'd come to see the elephants, not look at statues.

Next, we were show into a museum of sorts. It was full of old junk, including coins, costumes and more statues. There was also a whole load of small golden Buddhas for sale. We pretended to be interested in the coins for a few moments (just enough time to give the old man who worked there a handful of rupees for his effort at pointing at things) and then motioned that we were ready to see the elephants.

The tuk-tuk driver nodded. "Come."

Clearly, the driver was a man of little words, but we followed him around the other side of the temple where a pitiful sight awaited us. Chained up, with a few large branches by its feet, was a young elephant. Another old man was standing near it with a stick. What the stick was used for we could only guess at. We stared at the poor creature, watching as it dragged the same branches back and forth, seemingly without purpose. We turned to leave, but the old man jabbered at us in a raised voice. Of course, we couldn't understand him, but it was clear he was asking for money. Annoyed, I handed him a few rupees and then followed the driver outside to the tuk-tuk.

5

Ten minutes later, there was still no sign of the elephants. Our driver was zipping along a busy road until he made a detour through a side street. "You want visit gem shop?" he asked, slowing down.

"No thanks," I said. "Just the elephants, please."

The man nodded and set off again. Soon we stopped outside another shop. "Many good souvenir. You want?"

"No," I repeated. "Just the elephants."

The man shook his head. "I already show you elephant. No more."

Just as we thought. The whole elephant thing had been a charade. Angela looked as annoyed as I did. I shook my head at our stupidity for falling for the ruse. I told the driver to return us to the hotel. He shrugged and set off. Less than ten minutes later, on the street parallel to our hotel, we pulled over. Without saying a word, I passed the man a five-hundred rupee note. The man brushed it away. "Price is 2000 rupee."

"What?" I exclaimed. "Two thousand? You must be joking. The price we agreed on was five hundred. Take it or leave it." Sitting next to me in the back, Angela looked embarrassed. She hated confrontations of any kind.

The driver shook his head. "But I show you around temple! I show you elephant! Other drivers charge 5000 rupees for same trip."

Somehow, I doubted that and I laughed, despite the gravity of the situation. Angela flashed me a look. "Just pay him," she whispered. "I want to go." I handed the driver the 500-rupee note and we both climbed out of his tuk-tuk.

"You pay more!" the driver demanded, drawing the attention of other tuk-tuk drivers parked outside the hotel. "You pay now!"

We ignored him and walked into the hotel. What a con-job it had been: lies from the very beginning.

6

After a quick bite to eat inside the sanctuary of the hotel, we decided to brave the outside world again. This time, instead of allowing ourselves to be hoodwinked on the streets of Colombo, we asked the hotel to summon a tuk-tuk for us. Angela wanted to visit a hotel-recommended shop to buy some gifts for people back home. The hotel staff duly obliged and five minutes later, we were introduced to a driver called Christen.

As well as speaking good English, he possessed the funniest laugh known to man. The first time we heard his hearty guffaw was on the way to his little yellow vehicle. He stumbled on a raised pavement, cart-wheeled his hands for a second before righting himself, and then burst into laughter. It was such an infectious cackle that we joined in too.

"I almost break my neck!" he said between chortles. "And I don't know why this is so funny!" He laughed again, shaking his head as if to clear the devilment inside. Finally subdued, he told us to climb aboard his tuk-tuk.

"I saw you arguing with other tuk-tuk driver," Christen told us. "Earlier in afternoon."

We told him about the promise of an elephant festival and that we had fallen for the ruse because of the so-called gardener.

"Did he say he worked at the hotel?"

I nodded.

"Very common lie. The two men were working as part of a team. You were lucky to only pay five hundred rupees. Usually they get more."

We set off, and were soon zipping through shortcuts that only motorbikes and tuk-tuks could fit through. At the end of one street, we emerged into a busy road flanked with old buildings that had probably been grand and opulent, but now were dirty and run down. As in Delhi, the pavements outside them were cracked and worn, sometimes piled with rubbish. One startling difference between Colombo and Delhi, however, was the lack of crowds. In the Indian capital, people had been everywhere, pressed along every street and packed into every bazaar; in Colombo there was hardly anyone. We continued for a few minutes until we stopped outside a small shopping arcade. One large store was full of bags, scarves and the like, so, while Angela went browsing, I remained in the tuk-tuk so I could chat to Christen.

7

"I used to work in the Middle East," he told me when I mentioned we lived in Qatar. "In Kuwait I worked as a driver for a rich Arab family. That's how I learned to speak English. I got free accommodation and food but hated every minute. The teenage children all had phones, and they would ring me in middle of the night and say 'Drive us to Burger King' or 'Drive us to Dunkin' Donuts' or 'Do this and do that', and I would have to do it. Their parents did not care. After seven years I could not take it any longer—"

"Seven years?" I was incredulous that Christen had put up with it for so long.

"Yes, seven years! But I needed the money. So, after Kuwait I went to Dubai and worked in a hotel. But I was an illegal worker and the authorities soon found me. I was deported back to Sri Lanka about five years ago. Then I became a tuk-tuk driver."

Christen told me that at first he worked for another man, a friend of the family who owned a small fleet of tuk-tuks. "I was grateful to this man, but I could not earn much money by working for him, so I saved every spare rupee I could until I had enough money to buy my own tuk-tuk. It was a proud moment for me and my family – to own something that would provide an income for us. It was a dream come true."

I asked him how much tuk-tuks cost.

"A new tuk-tuk in Sri Lanka cost maybe $3500! Very expensive! But mine cost $1800. I bought it from someone I know, so got special price."

Angela came out with a bagful of goodies: a few silk scarves, some small wooden elephants and a green sarong. "The sarong is for any temples we might visit," she said, joining me in the back of the tuk-tuk. "I'm sick of wearing the ones they provide. I should've bought one a long time ago."

Christen dropped us off in an area of Colombo known as Fort, located only a short walking distance from our hotel. After thanking him, and paying him a generous tip, we wandered along the sea promenade towards the Galle Face. Apart from a few cannons pointing seawards, there was nothing left of the old Dutch fort; the British had seen to that. When the British had taken over in the early nineteenth century, they had pulled down the defensive walls and demolished as many Dutch buildings as they could, replacing them with what they saw as fitting British developments. Still, the name stuck, and Fort is now the business end of Colombo, with a few skyscrapers, upmarket hotels, government buildings, and even the Sri Lankan president's residence – the large and colonial Secretariat Building. It was so grand that it was where Queen Elizabeth II used to stay when she was on her state visits to Ceylon. Angela and I walked near it, trying to imagine the opulence of a time gone by. The residence looked distinctly colonial, full of columns, proud verandas and palm trees, but like most buildings in Sri Lanka, its smog-blackened roof and occasional cracked tile meant it was showing its age. As we passed a flea-bitten dog lounging in the shade of a cannon, we stopped to stare down into a dirty green inlet that lapped against the rear of the Secretariat Building. From a distance, the water had looked inviting, but up close we could see piles of rubbish floating in it, mainly rotting vegetables. The stench soon had us on our way.

For the remainder of the day, we lounged by the salt-water pool at the Galle Face Hotel, basking in the sun of a tropical Sri Lanka. Tomorrow promised to be an early start. We were going to Sri Lanka's second city, Kandy.

Top row: The Indian Ocean, as seen from the Galle Face Hotel; Me about to blast the enemy
Middle row: Sri Lankan rupees; The old Dutch Fort area, now the modern part of Colombo
Bottom row: The Secretariat Building; Me posing in front of an arresting statue

Chapter 8. Kandy Crush

The alarm clock went off at 5.30am. It was still dark. The last time we'd been up so early had been in Nepal, but, this time, instead of climbing a mountain to watch the sunset, we were going to be sitting in an air-conditioned car as we drove to the city of Kandy, Sri Lanka's ancient capital. En-route, we would make a slight detour to visit Pinnawala Elephant Orphanage, home to almost ninety elephants, but the downside, apart from the early start, was that the journey to Kandy – even though only 73 miles – would take at least four hours. It promised to be another carnival of beeping, overtaking and death-defying swerving.

By the time our car set off, the sun was making an appearance, casting a warming glow over the long sea promenade, as well as reflecting off the skyscrapers in the distance. Despite the early hour, the tuk-tuk drivers were all out in force, parked near the entrance of the Galle Face, and I wondered whether the gardener and 'government-approved' driver were around. It was probably too early for their little double act.

Our driver was a man in his early forties called Prasad. He preferred to keep conversation to a minimum, but we didn't mind as we threaded our way out of the city and into the countryside. Outside said it all: a man poking about in some smoking embers with a short stick, a woman carrying a basket of eggs on her head, a storekeeper hanging up small bananas outside his hut; the images outside were enough to keep us entertained.

As we drove through a small town, Prasad spoke for the first time in a long while. "You want stop? Maybe to go toilet? Maybe have drink? I know somewhere nice. Tourists always stop and say very nice."

I looked at Angela. She looked keen, and so we turned into a small car park next to a three-storey building. The small café served milky sweet tea on a veranda overlooking jackfruit trees and rickety village buildings. Behind the village was pure jungle, an endless expanse of green that stretched until the haze took over.

"I'm knackered," I announced, taking another slurp of the sickly-sweet tea. It was even sweeter than the tea we'd had in the carpet shop in Delhi.

"You always are if you get up before sunrise."

"That's because it's not natural – and neither is this." I pointed at the fish eye on my knee. "It's really worrying me. So I've decided to do something. If it looks no better tomorrow, I'm going to do something about it. Better than letting it hatch of its own accord."

Angela opened her mouth as if she was going to say something, but then closed it again.

I said, "I'm going to squeeze it really hard and if that doesn't do anything, I'll get a hot needle and poke it to death."

My wife looked disgusted, and well she might, because the thought of doing it horrified me too. God only knew what would come out after puncturing the cornea with a needle. I grimaced in Angela's direction. "So prepare yourself for horror in the morning, that's all I'm saying."

Our car journey with Prasad carried on, taking us through the uplands of central Sri Lanka. Because we had commenced our journey from Colombo so early, we were now seeing the start of morning traffic rush – delivery trucks, over-laden motorbikes and the ubiquitous tuk-tuk. School was due to start too, because troops of teenage girls wearing long white uniform-dresses were walking along the dusty verge, laughing and joking as they passed busy fruit stalls.

Beyond the buildings was thick green jungle, the abode of roosting fruit bats. Hundreds of them dangled from one tree's branches like black, leathery fruit. Why they had chosen that particular tree, we couldn't fathom. An hour later, Prasad announced that we were close to the elephant orphanage.

2

The Sri Lankan Department of Wildlife Conservation founded the Pinnawala Elephant Orphanage in the mid-70s. They had to: people had been decimating elephant habitats for years, forcing the animals to search further afield for food. The elephants often stumbled upon agricultural land, damaging and devouring crops, and so farmers began killing them. Then the terrible civil war started in 1983, a conflict that would last for another quarter of a century. With government forces pitted against Tamil Tiger troops, elephants were inevitably caught in the crossfire. Between 1990 and 1994 alone, 261 of the animals were killed.

The orphanage has become a lifeline to many of Sri Lanka's unweaned elephants, with teams of *mahouts* caring for their every need. These teams walk them, bathe them and feed them, which, for almost a hundred elephants, is no mean feat. Every single day, the herd needs six tons of assorted jackfruit, coconuts and greenery.

When adults reach maturity, they are sold to private owners or temples. A few are kept at the orphanage as part of an ongoing breeding program, but none will ever be released back into the wild; they are all too dependent on humans. Two elephants, however, are permanent residents. A male elephant called Raja is blind, and a female elephant called Sama only has three legs. Her fourth was blown off after she stepped on a landmine.

Prasad parked the car, got us some tickets, and pointed up a slight hill, telling us to walk there. At the top of the hill were a few gawping tourists, and, when we joined them, we saw why. Below us, in a slight meadow, was a herd of elephants chomping away on piles of leaves, or else standing head to head, staring at each other. Many looked fully-grown, but there were enough little ones with flapping ears to make us all coo. A few mahouts were dotted among the herd, gesturing that we should come down and stroke them.

Angela and I approached an elephant at the edge of the group. It didn't look fully-grown, but it did seem capable of causing serious harm if it was so inclined. Thankfully, it looked good-natured and allowed me to stroke its head without any fuss. Angela asked the young mahout whether it was a male or female.

"Adolescent female," he answered. "All elephants here are female, except baby ones." He pointed to our left. "Adult males over there. They do work. Drag logs, maybe carry things. You will see."

Angela stroked the elephant's head and trunk, and I took a picture. I noticed that its eyes were following my movement, showing intelligence and perception. How anyone could kill one of these creatures was beyond me.

We walked to where the mahout had pointed, and, around a corner, saw a young male elephant dragging a large log across a boggy field. It looked happy enough, though, and its task did not seem overly onerous, but, even so, compared to the lady elephants munching away in the sun, free to roam where they pleased, it didn't seem fair. The mahout in charge told us that if the males were allowed to wander, then the females would be constantly harassed. It was easier and safer for all involved to keep them separate.

We noticed a rush of people heading down towards the nearby river. Apparently, the elephants would soon be making their way down there to bathe. The mahout told us to go and watch. "This is best part of day for the elephants," he said. "This is when we see them smile."

3

"Look at the size of that thing!" I said, as a large male elephant plodded past. Angela and I, together with all the other visitors, were waiting behind barriers to allow the elephants to parade past. "It's got two bloody trunks!" Angela laughed. The elephant's mammoth member was perhaps two feet long, dangling there for all and sundry to see. It was thicker than my thigh. No wonder the males were kept separate from the females.

Another few males came along with their mahouts, but none seemed quite as well-endowed as the big boy. Then the female herd came: each and every one looking forward to bath time. Some were chuffing along at top speed, and their green-shirted handlers were only managing to keep a lid on a stampede by whacking a few of the more errant ones with sticks.

When it was deemed safe to do so, everyone followed the last of the elephants along a dusty trail leading down to the river. Because it was such a tourist draw, souvenir shops and cafes were conveniently located along both edges of the track. At the bottom, one large restaurant overlooked a wide expanse of river, and its verandas were packed with camera-toting tourists clamouring for the best spot.

Angela and I elected for a vantage point on the riverbank, staring at the eighty or so elephants wallowing in the shallow water. A few mahouts were washing some elephants, while the rest of the herd waited their turn, flapping their large ears as they found a spot to bathe. A few elephants lay sideways in the water, allowing their mahouts easy access to their hides for a good scrubbing. It was a scene of unrivalled elephant joy, clearly the highlight of their day.

"You want palm reading?" said a hopeful voice.

The small, thin man in his sixties was looking up at us expectantly. I told him no, thank you.

"Maybe later?"

I shook my head and he waltzed off into the crowd. Another palm reader tried his luck, as did a peddler from a nearby shop. But we were only interested in the elephants, as was everybody else. We all stood there and watched the spectacle until it was time for the elephants to leave.

4

We found Prasad reclining in his car seat, asleep and snoring. His door was open, so I coughed in his direction, which awakened him with a jolt. Five minutes later, we were back on the road towards Kandy: only an hour away, Prasad promised.

The main highway from Colombo to Kandy was little more than a winding, two-lane strip of dusty tarmac. In front of us, a large diesel-swilling truck coming in the opposite direction had crossed into our side of the road. It was going 1mph faster than the bus it was overtaking, and any fool could see it would never make it in time. Prasad didn't seem overly concerned, however, and made no attempt to slow down as the truck bore down upon us. Just when a collision seemed unavoidable, Prasad swerved onto the roadside verge, sending a plume of dust in our wake and causing chickens to run for cover. As the truck hurtled past, Angela looked up. Both of us read the slogan printed above the driver's window: JESUS SAVE ME, it stated. Yes, indeed.

Kandy was a crush of honking tuk-tuks, surrounded by crowds of people, all set around a line of souvenir shops. It certainly was not the tranquil mountain town we'd expected. That said, it did have a gorgeous lake and a whole raft of temples shrouded in dense vegetation.

Its tropical location made it the ideal location for the 1984 film, *Indiana Jones and the Temple of Doom*. The producers had originally wanted to shoot the movie in northern India, but the government there had refused permission, deeming the movie racist and offensive. The crew flew to Sri Lanka instead and set up camp in Kandy for a few weeks.

Long before that, British colonialists had discovered Kandy, and liked it so much that they took over. Unsurprisingly, the locals, not too happy to have tea-sipping Brits in their midst, rebelled. Their leader was a man called Keppetiploa Disawe.

Disawe's men described him as an incredibly brave fighter, even though they did acknowledge he had an odd face– it was freakishly wide for one thing. This didn't stop him rousing the spirits of a fellow chieftain in joining in with the rebellion and, by October 1817, a full-scale uprising against British rule was soon in full swing.

With impeccably bad timing, however, Disawe contracted some terrible disease, rendering him bedbound, and the British captured him. They sentenced him to death by beheading. On the block, after chanting a few poems, he asked his executioner to give him one swift blow to the neck to end his suffering quickly. The man with the axe nodded, but the first swing missed the mark, severing arteries but not delivering a death blow. The second swing did the job and Disawe was finally dispatched. The British, who had noticed his strange, wide face, sent the poor man's skull back to England for analysis.

Meanwhile, the rebellion continued, but the British proved horrendously efficient at quelling what remained of it. Tearing around the Kandyan countryside, well-armed British troops killed thousands of men they suspected were rebels, and then set fire to villages, systematically killing their livestock in the process. In the face of such violent attacks, the uprising petered out; its rebel leaders captured and sent to the chopping block. To finish off the job, and to make sure nothing like it ever happened again, British forces took over a Kandyan village called Uva. They rounded up every male over the age of eighteen and killed them without mercy. After that, no one dared to question British rule. As for Disawe's skull, the British finally returned it to Sri Lanka in 1954, and its arrival caused great celebration in Sri Lanka. Fittingly, his skull travelled to Kandy, where it now sits buried under a memorial.

6

Almost everyone who visits Kandy will see the Temple of the Tooth at some point – one of the most sacred places in Buddhism because it supposedly contains an actual tooth of Buddha. After being dropped off next to a large artificial lake (where a monk was talking to someone on his mobile phone), Angela and I made our way to it.

We removed our shoes and left them in the care of a bad-tempered and elderly shoe handler (who demanded a few rupees for the service) and then walked through the main temple entrance. Inside, a ceiling of gold awaited us, as did numerous statues of Buddha. One was so large that, to see it in its full glory, we had to circle it. An orange-robed monk, loitering nearby, tutted at us. When we looked over, he made a gesture that we were walking around the statue in the wrong direction.

"Where is the bloody tooth?" I asked Angela, a few minutes later.

"How would I know? You're the one with the map."

I looked at the pathetic map again. I'd printed it from the Internet before our trip, but might as well have printed a blank page for all the use it was. Compounding matters was the lack of signs telling us where to go. We traipsed through another corridor, passing a few pilgrims sitting on the floor. They were either having packed lunches or preparing offerings to Buddha, we couldn't tell. Fresh flowers lay in large piles everywhere, placed there by pilgrims who had passed through before us. A few people in front were depositing even more on the floor around the statues. As soon as they moved on, a temple cleaner brushed them into one of his messy but sweet-smelling piles.

The canine tooth was reportedly over two centuries old, extracted from the cremated body of Lord Buddha in India. Why and how it was removed, we didn't know, but we did know that as soon as people had it in their possession they started to believe it held magical properties. Whoever owned the tooth, they thought, would become ruler of the land. The upshot was that vicious wars were fought to take possession of the charred tooth, but then something unexpected happened: instead of seeing the tooth as an extension of the Buddha, people began worshipping the canine itself. This angered hard-line Buddhists, who ordered that it be destroyed. Rampaging gangs of zealots went in search of the tooth, and came so close to finding it that a royal couple decided to save it. They did so by fleeing to Sri Lanka, where the tooth ended up in Kandy in the Temple of the Tooth.

Angela and I arrived at a hellish crush of people. They were all shuffling towards what looked like a partitioned area guarded by curved elephant tusks. A few guards loitered nearby, making sure the queue kept moving, and very quickly we were being jostled from all directions. When we reached the front, we were disappointed to find we couldn't even see the tooth. It was hidden behind an embroidered curtain. Later, we would find out that only special dignitaries got to go behind the curtain. After being pummelled in the kidneys for the tenth time, I decided enough was enough; Angela agreed, and we left the Temple of the Tooth, stepping back into the sunshine and humid heat of a Kandyan morning.

7

Hawkers were out in force just outside the temple complex. They doggedly followed us along the street until they realised we were not going to buy anything. I could tell that Angela was interested in a few items, but since Nepal, she'd been forced to rein in her buying; the suitcases could not take much more.

The buildings around us were a mixture of faded colonial glory and bedraggled shops, travel agencies and jewellery emporiums. Many of the locals, we noticed, were carrying umbrellas as protection against the sun. To escape it ourselves, we headed towards a large white hotel.

Inside was dimly-lit but air-conditioned, and we chose some seats near a window in the empty bar area. A waiter had jumped up to attention as soon as we'd walked in, evidently surprised that he had customers. He took our order and silently backed away, smiling broadly.

"What do you think of Kandy?" I asked my wife.

Angela looked outside. It was grimy with the stains of the tropics. "It's okay," she said. "The lake is nice, and I love the lushness around. But that tooth thing was a big let-down."

I nodded, looking at the fish eye on my knee again. If anything, it had grown. It looked a cod eye ripe for bursting. I decided there and then that I couldn't wait until we got back to the hotel. It needed dealing with now. With my thumb and forefinger poised tentatively, I prepared to squeeze it as hard as I could.

"What are you doing?" asked Angela, "You're not messing with your spot, are you?"

I ignored her. The moment had come, and to hell with the consequences. I squeezed as hard as I could, and nothing happened. I squeezed again, and this time, quite horribly, a white, worm-like thing erupted from the centre. I almost gagged. I stopped squeezing and felt a wave of nausea wash over me.

I looked up at Angela. "Oh my God…"

"What?"

"Jesus Christ, it's…"

"*What?*"

"It's hatching…it's disgusting… I feel sick."

Angela's grimaced. "What's hatching?"

I looked at the worm, if it even was such a thing. It wasn't moving or anything – it was just sticking upwards, as if tasting the air for the first time. "Something came out."

My mouth was dry and I forced myself to peer closely at the thing. It looked like a long globule of dried white glue, the same type found in schools. I touched it and found it sticky but dry. I pulled at it and found that it stretched. I felt bile rising from the pit of my stomach.

"Leave it," ordered Angela. "Whatever you're doing, leave it! It's disgusting!"

"I can't leave it. It's sticking out of my knee. I'm going to pull it all out!" I tugged at the glue worm until it thinned and then snapped. I showed the carcass to Angela who gagged and closed her eyes. I scrunched it up in a napkin and then set to work on the rest. It was a nasty job, but now that I'd started it, I wanted to finish it one way or the other. I squeezed again and more white worm came out, and the more I squeezed, the more it oozed. It was like a well. A well from hell.

"Stop," hissed Angela. "Here comes the waiter."

I quickly brought my hands up to the table and whistled.

The waiter deposited a silver tray containing a teapot, two cups and a small bowl of sugar cubes in front of us. Then he backed away again, smiling all the way. When he was gone, I continued with my grim work.

"Jason," whispered Angela, looking about as aghast as I'd ever seen her, "please stop."

"In a second." I gritted my teeth and gave the hardest squeeze ever. A globule of white shot out, followed by a bit of blood, but I'd finally got to the end of the worm. I dabbed the wound with another napkin and sat back in my seat. "It's done," I said, wiping my brow. "The beast is dead."

Angela looked at me for a good while. "Why do you have to be so disgusting all the time?"

8

With a plaster covering my worm hole, Angela and I had a walk around the lake. Unlike the rush and push of the main streets, the lakeside was serene and calm. Long necked birds stood agilely on almost-submerged tree branches, and people walked arm in arm around the shaded and leafy path that ran alongside the water. Angela and I stopped to take a photo of the green, almost still, water.

"So what's the plan for tomorrow?" I asked. "We've done most of Colombo. I suppose we could always relax by the pool."

Angela swatted away a buzzing thing, probably a mosquito. We'd heard plenty of their shrill, high-pitched buzzes as they swept past our ears, and, now that she'd seen first-hand what a bite from a strange creature could do, she was more wary. "I think we should go on another train."

"A train?"

"We both enjoyed that one in Delhi. I think we should go on a Sri Lankan train journey."

"To where?"

Angela shrugged. "To anywhere. It doesn't matter. Let's throw caution to the wind and fly along the rails. When we get back to Colombo tonight, we can buy a map and see where the trains go. It'll be a mini-adventure in our big adventure."

"Have you lost your mind?"

"No. I just think it will be fun. Like you said, there's nothing else to see in Colombo."

My mind computed the logistics of it all. The issue wasn't so much about the train, but about where to stay. Hotels had always been pre-booked weeks beforehand. And now Angela wanted to leave the path and go off-road. We would be backpacking. "What if we can't find somewhere to stay for the night?" I asked.

Angela smiled. "We will."

"What about luggage?"

"We'll take a bag with enough things for one night."

"You've thought this through."

"Not really. I just think it will be better than hanging around by the hotel pool all day. We can do that in Qatar."

An hour later, as we threaded our way back to Colombo with Prasad, I thought more about Angela's plan. It *was* exciting to go somewhere on the hoof, so to speak, especially in a place as beautiful as Sri Lanka, and as the sun dropped below the horizon, and the bats began to hunt, I realised I was looking forward to it. When we arrived at the Galle Face and pored over a plastic-coated hotel map that showed the rail routes throughout the country, I grew more excited. A town on the southern tip of Sri Lanka stood out. It was the namesake of the hotel: Galle. That would be our destination.

Top row: Jack fruit we saw in the café on the way to Kandy; A teenage tuk-tuk driver trying to entice a customer
Middle row: A monk stands by Kandy Lake; street of downtown Kandy
Bottom row: The entrance to the Temple of the Tooth; I never knew that elephants could have two trunks

Chapter 9. The Slow Train to Galle

The next afternoon, Angela and I caught a tuk-tuk to Colombo's Fort Railway Station. After negotiating the ticket booths, where fat, five-abreast queues had merged into one massive mob, we managed to buy ourselves one-way tickets, second-class, to Galle, at a cost of 180 rupees each (83p). Return tickets were not allowed, we were told. We'd have to buy them at the other end.

"What about first class?" I asked the man behind the hatch. He was already dealing with someone else, an elderly lady who seemed to be buying enough tickets for ten families to go on every Sri Lankan train for the next decade.

The man looked at me irritably. "First class gone."

"Okay, do we have assigned seats in second class?"

"No seat, sir," he wasn't even looking at me now; instead he was counting out the pile of dirty crumpled notes the old woman had passed him. "When train come, push hard, otherwise may not get seat. Very busy train."

I thanked him and asked which platform the train left from.

"Five," he barked. "Train leave at 2.50pm. Express train."

I glanced at my watch. It was only quarter past two, so we still had plenty of time, but not enough to go wandering. We thanked the man again and headed to the platform.

The Fort Railway Station looked similar to Delhi's, most notably because it was large, dirty and noisy. Gaps in the wrought iron canopy above our heads allowed shafts of light onto the platforms, emphasising the cracks and ruts. Below us, the tracks looked rusted and worn.

"How long will the journey take?" Angela asked, trying to ignore the stares we were getting.

"Three hours, I think," I said. I was looking at a trio of men taking a shortcut across the tracks. Did they not realise they were dicing with death?

At 2.20, with a great blast of its deep resonant horn, an old blue diesel train pulled up. Before it had even stopped, almost everyone surged forward. Remembering the ticket seller's advice about the lack of seats, we joined the scrum, pushing towards the still-moving train.

The train came to a standstill with a hiss of its old brakes and then the doors opened, causing a second surge. It was madness; there was no other way to describe it. Departing passengers couldn't get off, no one could get on; each door was a bottleneck of humanity. I looked at Angela and shook my head. My face was sweating with the heat and the exertion, but somehow the plug was removed and someone managed to climb out of the train, dragging his belongings with him. It was as if a cork had been popped. A stream of people was now climbing out into the cloying atmosphere of the platform, and a second stream was fighting its way in. There was no order to how it worked. How no one was injured was a miracle.

We were still a few metres from the open door and I shouted to Angela, who had managed to get slightly ahead of me, that she should just go for it. "If you get on before me, save a seat!"

Angela nodded, and a few seconds later, she mounted the steps, squeezed into the doorway and disappeared from sight. I was close behind, but my backpack was hindering my progress. It was like an anchor dragging me back in the sea of people. I lunged forward, physically moving a man out of the way so I could climb aboard. He couldn't complain, as he was doing the same thing to someone else. I heaved myself up the steps into the passenger compartment and found Angela frantically trying to save me space on a blue plastic seat. I jumped into it just in time. Angela looked at me and shook her head. Then she laughed; I did too. We had done it! We had boarded the train!

A few minutes later, at just after half-past two and with another blast of its horn, the train pulled away from platform 5.

2

"Is this the right train?" I asked Angela.

"What do you mean?"

"I hope we're on the right train."

Angela's face looked confused. "Why wouldn't it be?"

Outside, we were passing over a clogged-up river and some shanty area of downtown Colombo. Even the palm trees could not mask the grime. "Because it left twenty minutes early. I thought that was a bit odd at the time…"

Angela began to look worried.

I asked the Sri Lankan woman next to me if we were on the correct train to Galle. She nodded and smiled: the smile of a person who didn't understand. I sat back, noticing an old man peering intently at me. "Train to Galle?" I asked. The mad nodded and smiled.

The train was trundling along at a slow pace, but the draught from the open windows provided some welcome relief, sending currents of cooling air into the stifling cabin. Women with infants in their laps took up most of the blue seats, but enough people were standing to remind me of the London Underground – only a friendlier version. In fact, the atmosphere aboard seemed jolly, full of chatty conversation and laughing. Almost everyone we made eye contact with smiled. Then the train slowed and stopped at another station, this one much smaller and less busy than Fort Colombo. No one got off, but a few people got on. I looked at Angela. "Should the express train stop like this?"

Angela didn't reply. She was watching a man wearing a sarong walking along the carriage. He had stopped more or less opposite us, gripping onto the rail running down the centre of the carriage. He looked at Angela and grinned, then looked at me and grinned. I grinned back, which made him grin some more. The man behind him swivelled his head so he could grin too. The woman next to me was grinning. Everybody was happy, so that was all right.

The train moved on again, and, as Colombo receded into the distance, a view of the Indian Ocean on one side and tropical jungle on the other filled the windows. This meant we were heading in the right direction, at least. As the journey continued, people's stares grew less obtrusive, and, at one point, the woman next to me offered us a cup of tea from her flask. We thanked her but declined, showing her our water bottles.

Occasionally, we passed dwellings that had clearly sprung up since the devastating tsunami of December 2004; faded signs near them read: Tsunami Relief Zone. It was along this stretch of coastline that a major tidal wave had surged, destroying everything in its path, killing 30,000 people in the process, and displacing another half a million. One particularly horrific incident involved a train, possibly very similar to ours, that had been travelling on the same stretch of railway.

3

The doomed train had begun its journey, like ours, at Fort Colombo railway station. As passengers boarded, carrying gifts for loved ones, looking forward to seeing family and friends, they were unaware of the seismic activity occurring thousands of miles away.

Because it was the Christmas holidays, the train was busy. According to the passenger manifest, between 1000 and 1500 paid passengers had crammed themselves into the eight carriages, but hundreds more had managed to sneak aboard without paying. At a few minutes before 7am, the train began its slow journey to Galle.

Far across the Indian Ocean, 160km off the coast of Indonesia, the seabed was rippling and cracking. Then, in one dramatic tectonic event, the bottom of the sea rose by several metres. This sudden uplift displaced unimaginable amounts of water, triggering tsunamis on the surface. Unsurprisingly, the first waves hit Indonesia, with Bangladesh and Thailand soon to follow. India and

Sri Lanka were next, and, at about 9.30am, approximately one and half hours into the train's journey, the waves made landfall along Sri Lanka's coast.

At first, it wasn't so bad. It was just a steady flood of seawater rather than the classic, crashing waves of people's imagination. Even so, because the tracks ran so close to the ocean, water quickly pooled around the train, bringing it to a standstill on the rails. As bewildered passengers looked to see what was happening, water began seeping into the carriages, starting to slosh around their feet. A nearby village was also under attack from the water, and the locals, believing the train would offer better protection, climbed onto its roof.

Meanwhile, just out to sea, worse was on its way. A towering, eighteen-foot wave of churning oceanic water was rapidly speeding towards them. As people battled with the rising floodwater inside their carriages, it crashed ashore. Such was its force that it lifted the train from the tracks and smashed it against some nearby trees. Wrecked carriages were soon engulfed in water, and one witness later described the wave as a cliff face. In the carriages, those who had survived the initial crash were now trapped, aware of the rapidly rising water around them. How they felt, as water rose above their chests, their necks and then their faces, is terrible to even contemplate. With no means of escape, hundreds of men, women and children drowned, and those that did manage to flee were quickly swept back out to sea. In just the space of a few minutes, the train was submerged beneath nine feet of water.

Miraculously, about twenty people survived. But for the other 1700 passengers, they died in the worst train disaster in history.

4

The train that Angela and I were travelling in started slowing down at another small station. A large placard on the wall told us we were in a place called Panadura. Even before the train had stopped, people started to climb off through the open doors, crossing the tracks into the fields beyond. When we stopped at the station, only a handful of people remained. One of them was an old woman, and when she saw that we were making no move to leave, she gestured that we should follow, babbling away and pointing to the exit. We got up and followed her down the steps but stopped when she left the platform. Instead, we doubled back and found a small, fly-ridden room where a station guard was sitting reading a newspaper. When he looked up, I asked him whether he spoke English.

"A little," he said.

Angela inquired about the next train to Galle.

"Galle? Train leave for Galle in two hours."

Two hours! But we had been on the fast train!

The man asked to see our tickets, and when we passed them over, he laughed. "These are express tickets! You get wrong train! Come back in one hour thirty minutes."

I looked at Angela and sighed. Our adventure had gone wrong at the first hurdle, but we decided to make the best of it. We would explore Panadura and then continue on to Galle with the next train. There was nothing else we could do.

We thanked the station guard and headed in the same direction that the old woman had gone. We crossed the railway tracks and then followed a sandy trail that opened up into a beach area full of families enjoying the sun. The woman was no longer in sight. Coconut trees swayed in the light breeze and a lapping ocean gently rolled in against the sand. It was idyllic, except for the people peering at us, plainly wondering what we were doing in their midst. There were so many people that I reckoned it must be some sort of public holiday or something. We turned onto a thin road, devoid of traffic, that ran parallel to the beach, aware of all the people staring openly. It became so unnerving that when we arrived at a small hotel called the Navro Beach Resort, we decided to go in.

5

"What would you like to drink, sir?" asked one of the four waiters who stood by our table. All of them had appeared as soon as we'd taken our seats at the rear of the hotel, near the empty swimming pool. We were the only guests, and our sudden arrival had caused a ripple of excitement.

"Do you have Lion Beer?" I asked, naming the most popular beer in Sri Lanka.

The waiter nodded and smiled. "We have many Lion Beers!" His three chums beamed like galoots, making me speculate whether we were the first Westerners to visit the hotel. When Angela ordered a glass of white wine, it caused some serious deliberation amongst the delegation. Angela looked embarrassed at ordering something so confusing, but eventually the first waiter nodded and bowed. "Beer and the white wine, sir. Is this the correct order?"

I nodded, and they wandered off in procession.

Five minutes later, seven waiters appeared by the doorway of the hotel. When I waved, all of them waved back. It was like being in a goldfish bowl. When the drinks came, they parted to allow the lead waiter passage. He placed Angela's glass of wine in front of her, opened my bottle of beer and then stood waiting. So did all the other waiters by the doorway. Angela took a sip and smiled. I took a swig and nodded my head. The waiter grinned, and everyone else grinned, and, after we'd grinned, the head waiter retreated to the doorway with his pals.

"This is so embarrassing," whispered Angela a few minutes later, leaning in close. "Are they still staring?"

I glanced over. "Yes. All of them."

Angela laughed nervously. "How long before we have to be back at the station?"

"One hour."

"Oh my God."

6

We wandered back out onto the beach area. Once more, people stopped whatever they were doing (which was mainly walking or playing on the sand with their children) to gawp. This time, instead of being embarrassed or uneasy about being the centre of attention, we tried to embrace it. What else could we do? We waved, and received waves back in return, smiled and received grins, and, as we walked onto the sand towards the ocean, people swivelled their heads to watch our progress. One toddler giggled as we passed.

At the water's edge, Angela and I regarded the beach. It was a long, thick wedge of golden sand, flanked by palms at one end and the town at the other. A young man, walking with a little boy, was heading in our direction. He looked as if he might change his mind at any moment, but in the end, no doubt helped by our smiles, he committed himself. With the population of the beach looking on with great interest, he stooped opposite us.

"Hello," he stammered nervously, "You American?"

His English was laboured but easily understandable. His son was watching us intently, his impossibly white teeth filling a small inquisitive face.

"No," Angela said, "English."

The man's eyes widened. "England! Football and Manchester United! I watch!"

We nodded and smiled. English football traversed all cultural barriers, it seemed; I'd had similar conversations with all sorts of people in many countries about Manchester United. Everybody in the world, from the richest man to the poorest man, had heard about Wayne Rooney. We all studied each other for a moment, and, while we did, a few more people approached, hovering in the distance, close enough to hear but not take part in the conversation.

"You stay in hotel?" the man said, flicking his gaze to the Navro Beach Resort.

'No. We catch train to Galle."

"Ah, Galle. Very nice! Big city!" The little boy was tugging at his father's hand, clearly bored with what was going on, so the man invited us over to where his wife was sitting. "We have…big rice and big roti! You can have!"

How amazing, I thought. A man offering to share his food with a couple of strangers he'd just met on the beach. It had happened on the train, too – the woman who had offered us some tea – it was generosity beyond all expectations. I could not imagine many people in the UK striking up a conversation with a foreign stranger, and then offering to share a meal with them. We thanked the man, but declined, telling him we had a train to catch. He nodded and smiled, and watched as we made our way off the beach.

7

It was dark by the time we arrived in Galle, but after commandeering a tuk-tuk to take us to a nice hotel we eventually arrived at the quite beautiful Lady Hill Hotel, a small boutique establishment located at the top of a winding hill. For the remainder of the night, we relaxed on our gecko-friendly balcony, watching as fruit bats hunted over a sea of black shadowy palms. The sound of chirping insects and eerie bird calls was the perfect accompaniment to a glass of white wine.

In the sixteenth century, Galle, under Portuguese control, had been the main port in Sri Lanka. Spices, gemstones and ivory were plundered from the steamy interior, brought to the coast and then piled aboard wooden ships, bound for Europe. When the Dutch took over, they carried on with the same trade lines, but added fortifications to the port area. Galle Fort still stands today, and is the largest remaining fortress built by Europeans in the whole of Asia. It was somewhere Angela and I intended to visit.

"Look," said Angela, peering behind the curtains of our room the next morning.

I joined her at the window. Now that it was daylight, we could see the view in all its glory: tropical plants as far as the eye could see. They covered the hills and plateaus in a lush layer of green up to the horizon. In the near distance, smoke was rising almost vertically from somewhere deep in the jungle. It epitomised a steamy jungle, one where it was not difficult to imagine dinosaurs roaming free.

Half an hour later, we were making our way down the hill into Galle town centre. As in Kandy, the main streets were a shambolic collection of fabric shops, fried food stalls and parking spots for green tuk-tuks. There were stands selling pineapples, green bananas and others full of drying fish. Each stallholder had a set of weighing scales that looked as old as the fort we were on our way to see. Sitting under a crisscross of telegraph poles was a mangy-looking ginger tomcat chewing on something that could have been a chicken wing, but probably wasn't. In an upstairs shop window was a line of colourful children's dresses hanging from wire coat hangers. A woman noticed me staring and glared, the first unfriendly look I'd received in Sri Lanka since the elephant-scamming taxi driver in Colombo. I returned my gaze to ground level just as a tout approached trying to sell us some green and blue peacock feathers. We decided it was time to see the fort.

8

Tongue-flicking monitor lizards and eagle-eyed chameleons patrolled the ramparts, bastions and sea walls of the old Dutch fort. Whenever I tried to take a photo of one, it would skitter away, hiding in a crevice or disappearing in the shadow of the stonework.

As well as the lizards, young Sri Lankan couples were enjoying the seclusion of the extensive wall system. They sat underneath large umbrellas whispering sweet nothings to one another as they gazed out over the ocean below.

Galle Fort contained a whole raft of old buildings, including a church, a mosque and a lighthouse, as well as narrow streets full of Dutch and Portuguese-era houses. I was interested to discover that when the tsunami had struck Galle in 2004 the 40-foot fortress walls had provided some much-needed protection against the onslaught, but could not stop the water entirely. The ocean simply surged along the edge of the walls until there was a gap, and then rushed in, near Galle's cricket ground, which it shattered in an instant. The dreadful wave then carried on to Galle bus station, where it swept away buses like corks on a lake. By the time the torrent receded, over 2000 people were dead.

Thankfully, the water looked calm now: a blue ocean with a few rolling waves. It was impossible to imagine the horror that came from it that day in December, a Boxing Day tsunami that killed almost a quarter of a million people across 14 countries. In the shallows, below the tall white lighthouse, was a teenage boy standing knee-deep in the water, armed with a thin fishing pole and line. Clear water was lapping against a section of yellow sand near him, but, further out, a set of jagged and rocky protrusions showed us why the lighthouse was necessary. We watched the boy for a few moments but the heat became unbearable so we moved on to find shade.

In a café in downtown Galle, we ordered a couple of Pepsis each. It was almost time to catch our train back to Colombo, but we needed to cool off first. "How's your growth?" asked Angela.

"Fine," I said, peeling back a tiny portion of the plaster. "Healing quite nicely. Why?"

"Because I think you might have another one – on your face. Oh wait, it's your nose."

"Funny."

Angela put down her glass, causing the ice-cubes to jangle. "We should do this more often – go off on little side adventures, not know where we'll be staying. It adds a little bit of mystery to things, don't you think? A little of the unknown. I can see the appeal of backpacking a little bit."

I smirked. "Backpacking? As if you could stay in a flea pit, eating lentils all day, living off fifty pence a day while I braided your hair!"

Angela smiled. "You know what I mean."

And I could. Going off the itinerary sheet had been invigorating, and, as Angela had said before we'd even set off to Galle, it had been like a mini holiday within the holiday. The experience of a real train journey with the people of Sri Lanka, and chatting with them on their beaches, had been fulfilling in a way that arranged travel could not compete. Our little side adventure to the south of Sri Lanka had been a roaring success.

Top row: The tropical, steamy jungle view from our hotel window in Galle; Street scene in the old Dutch quarter
Middle row: Galle Lighthouse; The view from the open door of the train
Bottom row: Downtown Galle; The train station in Galle

Chapter 10. The Beaches of Beruwala

Our plan was to have a few days rest and recuperation before heading off to Bangladesh. To that end, we had factored in a three-day break, a chance to recharge our batteries, on a Sri Lankan beach.

The place we chose was Beruwala because, for one thing, it had plenty of hotels to choose from, and it was only one and a half hours south of Colombo by car. Better than all of that, though, Beruwala promised a palm-fringed getaway from the bustle of everyday life. Both of us needed a break after the frenetic activity of the last few weeks.

Beruwala began its life as an eighth century Arab trading post. Merchants from Arabia settled on the island, bringing prosperity and wealth with them. When Marco Polo visited a few hundred years later, he declared the island the finest in the whole world.

Around this time, Beruwala established itself as a haven for exotic medicines. Royalty from the Maldives visited regularly to receive treatment from herbalists. But then European colonists arrived, stripping the land bare and building their own walled quarters. Beruwala's glory days as a centre for medicine were over and the town reverted to fishing.

By the 1970s, tourists had discovered the beaches of Sri Lanka, including Beruwala's, and even the terrible Civil War couldn't stop them coming. Hotels were constructed, tourist infrastructure developed and towns, such as Beruwala, metamorphosed into service centres for wealthy visitors. Holiday brochures tempted them in their thousands.

Angela and I were staying in one of the western-style hotels that adjoined the beach. It was perfect. It even had a little beetle outside the room that flashed a luminous yellow light every few seconds – the first firefly either of us had ever seen. It was going to the perfect way to spend a few days.

2

Looking at the hotel, now, it was hard to imagine the damage caused by the Tsunami of 2004. I'd seen video footage on YouTube of that awful morning. The tourist who had shot the film was standing on a balcony overlooking the swimming pool. On the far left of the screen was a cluster of coconut palms, then the ocean, and above it, a gorgeous blue sky. It looked like another day in paradise. The time on his video camera read 10.29am.

The amateur cameraman focused on some hotel workers stacking chairs, others rushing hither and thither, all of them clearly aware of an approaching storm. Some of the workers were shouting at each other to hurry. Forty-nine seconds later, a brown trickle of water arrives through the palms, and lazily trickles into the swimming pool. Within seconds, hotel workers are scurrying through ankle-deep water around the edge of it. Two minutes in, and the water comes in faster, toppling the stacked white chairs. Pieces of debris start floating inland too, and, when the cameraman pans across to the pool, it is completely brown. A pile of matter has also collected around the low-level dining room at the far end of the pool, including, the cameraman notices, a carcass of a dead dog.

At 10.38am, less than ten minutes since the start of the footage, the camera leaves the swimming pool and points at the ocean. It focuses on the churning white wave rushing towards the shore. A minute later, the torrent erupts through the coconut trees and engulfs the whole area below the balcony. The place where the swimming pool used to be is now submerged under a foot of eddying water. Just then, the cameraman notices two hotel workers hanging onto a sturdy pillar, part of a pavilion-like building, while water rips around their waists. An almighty wave crashes over them and the men lose their grip. The camera swings across and finds them at the far end of the hotel complex where the deep end of the pool used to be; they are tumbling among the debris. A few seconds later, they right themselves and begin to swim to safety. The low-level restaurant, the one where the dead dog rests, is now in danger of being totally submerged. Then, at 10.43, just fourteen minutes into the drama, the water begins a retreat. It's as if a hellishly powerful suction device is out to sea, drawing the ocean back to where it belongs. As it recedes, the tsunami leaves behind a lake of foul-looking water, piles of broken chairs, water-soaked palm leaves and groups of bewildered people.

3

The next morning, Angela and I had our first real look around the hotel. As we made our way towards the open beach, we passed tourists reading their Kindles while they fried under the sun. Many of them, we were sure, would know little, if anything, of the tsunami that had hit Beruwala, and why would they? For the vast majority of Western tourists, Sri Lanka was a tropical destination to relax in, and not one to think about disasters. That was fine, I thought, but what was not, at least in my eyes, was that many of these European tourists would never set foot outside of the hotel grounds. To me, this was a tragedy.

"Look at the beach," chirped Angela. The scene was like a holiday brochure: palm-fringed and exotic. All along the shore, stalls were selling hats, saris, shells and turtle mats, and out across the surf was a small, overgrown island. It looked like the sort of place where Robinson Crusoe might have lived.

"Hello, sir," said an accented voice. It belonged to a small, thin-faced man wearing a brightly-coloured sarong. He had all the hallmarks of a beach hustler – shifty eyes, false smile and an armload of trinkets. "From England?"

We nodded, smiled and then walked away.

"You staying in Eden Hotel, sir?" he shouted after us.

Again, we nodded, but carried on with our wandering, not even bothering to turn around. Besides, it wasn't hard to work out where we were staying: the Eden was the nearest hotel.

The man trailed us. "Don't you recognize me, sir? I work at hotel as waiter. I serve you in morning. Remember?"

"Really?" I said, turning to face him. "What did I have?"

The man smiled. "Ah, I do not remember food, sir. But I remember you and lady. Very nice people!"

"The thing is, we didn't have breakfast this morning so you couldn't have seen us."

The man's eyes widened, but he quickly recovered. "Maybe yesterday morning. Yes! I remember now, yesterday."

Despite myself, I smiled; the man was harmless, and was only trying to make a few rupees. I looked at his wares: small wooden keyrings carved with people's names. I asked him how much they cost.

"Very good price, sir. Cheap! Just come to my small workshop, over there, at edge of beach, and my friend make for you."

I nodded. "Maybe later."

"Okay, maybe later. Hut is over there." He pointed and we looked. "Please remember."

After a wander along the beach, kicking the sand beneath our feet and taking a quick paddle in the warm ocean, we headed back to the hotel, stopping to buy a keyring along the way. The man was overjoyed to see us, as was his business partner, who worked diligently with a small chisel for a few minutes to produce a keyring with my name carved into it. Satisfied with the product, we handed over some rupees and entered the hotel grounds. While Angela went for a swim, I went to photograph lizards.

Ever since I was a child, I have been fascinated by lizards. Big, small, fat or thin, I love them all, and the bushes and quiet trails of the Eden Hotel were full of them. Small orange-yellow geckos hung from the sides of walls around the main buildings, while large brown skinks patrolled the tree trunks and flowerbeds. At one point, I came across a fearsome-looking monitor lizard trampling through some undergrowth near a maintenance shed, its tongue flickering this way and that as it tried to pick up a scent, but, when I approached, it scarpered, sending butterflies and pollen tumbling. Instead, I crept to a flowery bush to spy on a green chameleon. Its weird, all-seeing eyes soon had me clocked, and, with surprising speed, it scrambled across the thin branches until it found safety in the shadow of a wall. I gave up on my lizard hunt and went to find Angela. Ten minutes later, I was flopped out on a sun lounger powering up my Kindle.

4

That afternoon, we were back on the beach, walking towards a few boats moored in the shallows near the sand. A gaggle of local men waited near them under a parasol. The hotel had warned us not to accept boat rides with any of these men because they were not insured, and their boats often ran out of fuel, or worse sank.

We walked past the palms and stray coconuts, waving away a few hopeful hustlers. All of the men smiled and got to their feet as we approached the boats. I picked one man for the simple reason that he was sitting on the left. He was a wiry individual, about thirty, wearing a grey shirt and brown shorts. His name was Damith.

After explaining that we wanted to visit the mangroves, see some wildlife, and then be dropped off back at the beach, Damith told us his price. It was a tenth of what the hotel had quoted. When I asked him to show us his vessel, he took us over to a sturdy-looking blue and white boat with an outboard motor.

"Good boat," he said, grinning. "Best in Beruwala."

"So it won't sink," I joked.

The man seemed to appreciate my humour. "No sink. But maybe you fall overboard. Then shark gobble you up. Tasty meal!" He laughed and so did Angela. The other men saw that we'd been hooked and wandered back to their shady spot beneath a parasol. We climbed aboard Damith's boat.

5

More or less as soon as we set off, a grey and white-ringed sea snake skimmed across the surface of the water beside our boat: it was the most poisonous reptile in Sri Lanka, according to Damith. Above us soared a squadron of fish eagles, looking for barracuda. When we turned into a side tributary, Damith slowed and brought the boat to a standstill by an overgrown sandbank. A thick line of trees lay just beyond it.

"Shush," said Damith, putting his forefinger over his lips. He quietly climbed out of the boat and then did something surprising. At the largest of trees, he grabbed a low-lying branch and shook it. At first, we wondered whether he was trying to dislodge some fruit, but he wasn't – Damith was waking slumbering bats. Four or five bats emerged from the foliage, swooping and circling around the tree, probably wondering what was going on. So did we, but we watched nonetheless, amazed at how big the bats were. Damith was already climbing back into the boat and the bats were settling down again. We moved on along the river.

Passing under a large iron bridge, a grimy diesel train thundered across. A cacophonous low honk erupted from within its bowels, lasting for many seconds, sending white egrets scurrying for cover and shaking the foundations of the crossing. As a thick grey cloud of smoke was left it its wake, I wondered whether it was the same train we'd been on a few days previously.

"Water monitor!" said Damith. "Look!"

Plodding along on the sand was a huge lizard, its tongue darting here and there, oblivious to our interest. It must have been over six feet long and it looked like a crocodile. Compared to the one in the hotel grounds, this was a dragon. Dinesh turned off the engine and allowed us to float nearer. It flicked its tongue in our direction and waddled into the sea, disappearing from sight. It was the biggest lizard I'd ever seen.

We hit the mangrove swamps. Large grey roots poked out from the water like skeletal fingers, while branches dangled down to caress our heads. Eerie hoots and frantic rustling came from unseen parts of the forest – it was like being on a floating ghost train. Further ahead, sitting on a small wooden jetty, was an elderly woman wearing a sari. She was washing her hair with bucketfuls of river water. Nearby, masses of litter and debris were tightly compacted into the riverbank. Behind them were tree stumps and downed wooden fences.

"Tsunami damage," Damith told us. "Very bad. Many people lose boat and home."

An elderly man in a small wooden boat approached us. When he was alongside, Damith and the man chatted for a few seconds, and then the old man reached into his boat and produced a small crocodile – about a foot and a half long. Even though the creature's mouth was closed, I could still see its razor sharp teeth poking out. The man passed the crocodile into our boat and Angela handled it first, followed by me. I put it down on the side of the boat where it sat motionless. Damith gave the crocodile's mouth a little flick and the reptile opened its jaws wide, revealing a full complement of teeth. I was taken aback; I'd assumed its jaws had been taped shut.

"Put finger in?" asked Damith.

We shook our heads and he laughed. Instead, the old man passed a shrimp over. Damith placed it next to the crocodile and hastily removed his fingers. It was a good job, because half a second later, the croc grabbed it, swallowed it and resumed its statue-like pose.

After handing the reptile back to the old man (and paying him some rupees), Damith returned us to the beach. We thanked him for a wonderful boat trip, far better and far cheaper than the one we'd had in Kerala.

6

The local beer, Lion Beer, was a refreshing drink. The only problem was the price the hotel charged for it. As a way of countering this insanity, Angela and I walked into Beruwala town to see if I could buy some there.

The town itself was quite small, but it did have a contingent of cows causing momentary chaos when they decided to cross the main street. As chance would have it, we had timed our arrival with market day in Beruwala. The sounds of bartering and good-natured chatter filled the stalls. Small shacks, selling everything from T-shirts and fish to large tubs of nuts and spices, were busy with the locals of town. Next to the main stalls were pavement vendors, usually women, sitting with ancient weighing scales among piles of passion fruit, pineapples, melons and cassava. One stall was selling chicks. About thirty of them were huddled together in a cage, some peering out between the bars, all looking impossibly cute.

"It's amazing," I said, "how something so adorable can grow up into something so ugly."

"Chickens are not ugly."

"Well, they're certainly not beautiful. And neither are sheep. But lambs are."

Angela ignored me and walked over to a stall selling an array of bananas and pumpkins. Sitting on the ground next to it was an old man with a stump for an arm. He looked at us pleadingly as we approached the counter. Angela pointed at a bunch of bananas, showing the man in charge three fingers. He nodded, snapped the bananas off, weighed them and handed them over in return for a few rupees. The crumpled notes I received as change I handed to the old man with the stump. He took them graciously in his one remaining hand.

On the way back to the hotel, we found the alcohol store. Unlike the one in Kerala, this one had an open counter that overlooked the street, and the young man working there was affable and chatty, talking about how nice Lion Beer was, and what we had done so far in Beruwala.

"You been to lighthouse yet?" he asked.

We shook our heads.

"You must go. Climb to top. Very good view."

After paying for the bottles, we thanked the young man and headed back to the hotel.

7

"This was supposed to be rest and recuperation," I yelled above the racket. We were battering across the waves in a small boat on our way to Beruwala Lighthouse. "Now look!"

"I know," Angela shouted back, her hair cascading around her head, "but we'd be bored otherwise."

Suddenly, my cap flew off, whipped and then tossed into the froth behind. And then my stomach lurched as we ricocheted off a swell. A fraction of a second later, my innards jolted as we crashed back down. I couldn't take much more of this. I gripped the handrail tighter.

Ten minutes earlier, we had tried to locate Damith, but the men under the parasol told us he was having a day off. We doubted that, but had to accept their word. We hired another man instead, and told him we wanted to visit the lighthouse. We spent a minute or so agreeing on a price before setting off.

Spray was lashing my eyes, so I closed them. Another surge catapulted us into the air, the glorious lack of friction short lived as we smashed back down again. The boatman was a lunatic, that much was clear, but then, joyously, he slowed the engine and everything returned to normal. I opened my eyes to see a small island in front of us. Poking above the mango, cashew and coconut trees was a lighthouse. The boat stopped and we alighted. The sound of chirping insects and whooping birdcall filled our ears. It was a perfect tropical island.

"You want to go inside lighthouse?" asked our boatman, as he dragged his vessel onto the sand. We looked up at the white structure and nodded, so he led us along a circular pathway towards it. A couple of bare-chested men wearing shorts were lounging in the shade near the lighthouse, smoking cigarettes. To one side of them was a pile of coconut shells. The men jumped up and spoke to our boatman for a few seconds.

He turned to us. "They say they will take you up, but want to know if you want coconut first?"

We nodded.

One of the bare-chested men stamped his cigarette out and walked to a coconut palm. Without any equipment, he shimmied up the trunk, using his arms and feet, and when he reached the top, where the large leaves were, produced a knife and started hacking away. A few moments later, a coconut dropped to the ground with an audible crush of vegetation. A second coconut swiftly followed.

He returned with the large green coconuts and a dangling cigarette in his mouth. His pal took them, expertly cut them open, and then gave us a fresh coconut each. The liquid inside was cool and tasty. The same man who had chopped the coconuts up was sporting some strange white stripes across his face. They looked like plasters. Because of them, I couldn't shake the image of a dark-skinned Adam Ant. Instead of being a singer, he turned out to be the lighthouse keeper. He waited for us to finish our drinks and led us into the tall white tower.

8

"This from England!" Adam Ant stated proudly. He was pointing at some old machinery that looked held together with paint. Maybe it was, I thought; the British had built the lighthouse in 1928, and the machinery looked like the original workings.

We followed him up some spiral metal steps until we reached the top section where the light was. The keeper told us it went on at 6.30pm every day and went off at 6.30am the next morning. "But if foggy, we switch on early."

We stared at the light, more for the benefit of the lighthouse keeper than ourselves; he seemed so proud of everything. "Every ship going to Maldives pass this lighthouse," he told us. "We are very important to them!"

I asked him how long he'd worked at the lighthouse.

"Since twelve-years-old. Long time!"

I judged his age to be about forty, so that was almost thirty years working in the lighthouse. We stood at the railings, staring out across a sea of coconut palms until they met the ocean. On the other side of the bay was a thin sliver of beach, a line of shacks and then another dense stretch of palms, which carried on to the horizon. Something within the green layer caught my eye. It looked like a giant man.

"Buddha," the lighthouse keeper said. "Giant Buddha."

Both Angela and I strained to see it, but it was too far away to make out anything except for a yellow and white, vaguely man-shaped blob. "Can we visit it?" I asked.

The man with the white stripes across his face nodded. "Get tuk-tuk. Very easy."

We climbed back down and handed the man a pair of one hundred-rupee notes, which he took and stuffed into his pockets. We found our boatman and gave him the nod. It was time to head for the harbour.

9

Beruwala Harbour was a mass of brightly coloured fishing boats. On a slight headland stood the white Kechimalai Mosque, constructed, supposedly, on the spot where the first Arab trader had landed in Sri Lanka. The smell of fish became stronger as we approached the harbour's edge. Hundreds of small dried fish sat piled up along the jetty. We climbed out of the boat and paid the boatman for his time, waving away the fish vendors who were trying to attract our attention. We saw a parked tuk-tuk, and, after a bit of explaining where we wanted to go, set off. The Kasgoda Sea Turtle Conservation Project was only a few miles away.

"These turtles are one day old," said the man in charge of the turtle conservation centre. He told us he'd worked there for ten years, but the centre had been open for twenty. The man took us over to a large rectangular container that stood about a metre off the ground. He removed a metal screen to reveal a swarm of cute baby turtles paddling around on the surface of the water. They were all about six centimetres long.

"Please, pick one up," the man said, smiling. "They will not bite."

We did, and their tiny flippers caressed our palms. "What kind of turtles are they?" asked Angela.

"Olive ridley," he replied. "They have hatched here, and, after three days, we let them go back into the ocean. We do this at night. Hopefully one day the females will return to lay eggs of their own."

We followed the man to see some older turtles, some of them quite large. "These are green turtles." He pointed at a large turtle in a tank of its own. It was about a metre in length. "Pick it up, but be careful – very heavy!" It weighed a ton, and it was a real effort getting the turtle out of the tank, especially with its flapping flippers trying to flip me over.

"So why are these older turtles here?" I asked.

"Because they have been injured, caught in nets or sometimes saved them from markets. Fisherman brought in this one. We had to give him money, of course, otherwise he would have cooked and eaten it. Come, I show you turtle egg enclosure."

We arrived at a fenced-off, sandy enclosure with small wooden signs poking out of the sand. "This is where we bury any turtle eggs we find," said the man. "They are one metre down in sand, safe from predators. We buy eggs from local people for twenty rupees (10p) each, otherwise the eggs will be sold to market for food."

In another tank was a large white and light brown turtle: an albino. Its head, flippers and outer shell were white, with only the inner shell offering any brown. "For every half million eggs a female lays, only one will be albino," said the man. "Shell is very soft, so we cannot let him go. Shark will eat him. But he likes tickles – watch."

The man put his hand in the water and began to tickle the shell of the white turtle. It immediately began to twist and turn with its flippers akimbo. It loved it and kept coming back for more.

"Plastic bags are big problem," said the man. "Turtle see plastic bag floating in sea and think it is jellyfish. They eat plastic bag and suffocate. Very sad."

On the way out, we left a healthy donation for the centre, hoping it would go some way to helping these amazing and extraordinary sea creatures.

10

The next morning was our last in Beruwala. Later that afternoon, we would be driving back up to Colombo, where we'd spend the night, before catching a hellishly early flight to Dhaka, Bangladesh, the final stop on our journey. So, to finish our trip to Sri Lanka, we hired another tuk-tuk so we could visit the Kande Viharaya Temple, the home of the giant Buddha statue we'd seen from the top of the lighthouse.

It turned out to be only five minutes from our hotel. As the car drove along a narrow road lined with shops and shacks, with dust tracks leading off into the hinterlands, we could see the massive structure jutting out above the tree line. We seemed to be the only motorized vehicle on the road; everyone else was either walking or riding old bicycles.

Our driver also acted as our guide. We clambered out of the tuk-tuk, wandered past an orange-robed monk tending to an elephant and walked straight up to the yellow and white Buddha. From somewhere came a loud cock-a-doodle-doo. I turned to see a rooster looking right at me. It cock-a-doodle-dooed again and then started pecking in the dust.

"That bird," said the tuk-tuk driver, "Always make big noise when he see me. Every time I come, he make noise like that. I think he hate me."

At 160ft (which is longer than a Boeing 737), Buddha was monstrously tall. And he was sitting down too. His droopy ear and half-closed eyes made him look like a classic Buddha, serene yet knowledgeable. Some stairs led to a walking platform around his base, and that's where we headed.

Flowers and small candles covered the edge of the platform, placed there by local people. At the rear of the statue, a fence overlooked pure jungle: green coconut trees as far as the eye could see. Beneath the Buddha was a temple. It was full of pictures and artwork depicting the life of the young Buddha, but empty of people. We didn't linger; instead we followed the tuk-tuk driver to another nearby building.

At the entrance, a sign warned us that photography was not allowed. It seemed a bit odd, I thought, especially since photography was permitted everywhere else. Wondering what delights awaited us, we stepped through the door.

It was a small and tatty museum. It didn't have anything to do with Buddha or Buddhist Temples; instead, it was full of old coins from around the world, the same type of thing seen in museums everywhere. Feeling duty bound, we had a quick look around and then made our way to the exit where we noticed a small man sitting behind a tiny desk. I was surprised we hadn't seen him on the way in. On the man's desk was a box, which read: donation, so

I fished around in my wallet and deposited a 50-rupee note in it. The man nodded and passed me a slip of paper written in Sinhalese. I had no idea what it said, but back outside, our driver translated it. "It say, thank you for donation, and wish you safe travel."

I stuffed it into my wallet as the cockerel crowed again. An hour later, we were back at the Eden Hotel packing our bags. This time tomorrow, I thought, we will be in Bangladesh.

Top row: Beach scene in Beruwala; Me holding a crocodile
Middle row: The Giant Buddha near our hotel; Angela posing on the balcony; me holding a day-old turtle
Bottom row: A man shimmying up a coconut tree at Beruwala Lighthouse; A massive water monitor lizard

Chapter 11. Dhaka, Bangladesh

Angela and I were the only westerners on board the flight to Bangladesh, but this did have an unexpected benefit on arrival at Shahjalal International Airport; there was no queue at the Foreign Passport Holders' immigration desk. Even so, we were both tired and irritable; our early morning departure from Colombo had been delayed an hour, and then another hour, and, by the time we had finally taken off, we'd been waiting around for almost seven hours.

"How long are you staying in Bangladesh?" asked the man with the stamp. He'd been studying our Qatari-issued visas for quite some time.

"Two days," I answered.

The man raised his eyebrows. "Only two days? Where stay?"

"Dhaka."

"And Dhaka is only destination in Bangladesh?"

"Yes."

The man glanced at Angela and then returned his eyes to me. "Two days not long enough to see beauty of my country. If you come again, make sure you visit Chittagong and Cox's Bazar. Both very beautiful. Much enjoy."

I told him we would and he stamped our passports to let us through.

2

By the time we had collected our luggage and stepped outside it was dark. It was also hot and humid, and I was thankful there was a line of taxis waiting just outside the terminal building. All we wanted was to get to the hotel so we could go to sleep and end the thoroughly miserable day. When air travel went as planned, it was just about bearable, but when it went wrong, it was a living purgatory.

Despite downtown Dhaka being only fourteen kilometres from the airport, it was taking an eternity to get there due to the giant, beeping traffic jam. In the back of the car, I huffed and puffed, straining to see what was going on.

"This normal traffic for time of day, sir," explained the driver, sensing my impatience. "Rush hour."

Outside, the lack of street lighting made it hard to see things beyond the beeping traffic. Dark buildings and even darker side streets gave the impression of a city under blackout conditions.

"No street lights?" I asked the driver.

"No, sir. Power cut. Government's fault. They shut down different parts of Dhaka at different times of day."

I peered at the indistinct buildings by the side of the main road, but all I could make out was faded Bengali script on some shop fronts. The only English I could see was on a restaurant called Yummy Yummy. It was pitch black dark behind the glass.

Buses, hands down, won the contest for the most dents, scrapes and missing tail lights. The one next to us was crammed to capacity with passengers, arms dangling from the open windows. Three people were sitting on the roof.

We moved forward fifty feet. A beggar took the opportunity to approach my side window. With his one good arm, he pointed to his stump. I tried to ignore him, even though the traffic wasn't moving anywhere, and, after a few seconds, he sloped off and was replaced by a girl of perhaps eight carrying a bundle of red roses. "Only ten taka for one piece!" she yelled through the glass. When I didn't look at them, she crossed to Angela's side. "Only ten taka, miss!"

Two hours after leaving the airport, we pulled up outside the hotel. From what our weary minds could gather, the Best Western La Vinci (why it wasn't called the Best Western *Da Vinci*, we couldn't fathom) was an oasis amid the chaos. We were soon asleep on the ninth floor, even managing to blot out the ceaseless beeping from the streets below.

3

The next morning, on our only full day in Dhaka before flying back to the Middle East, I opened the curtains to see the lay of the land. It was a shock. One side of my panoramic view was a hellish snarl of traffic, all squeezing and beeping their way along at less than a walking pace. The number of pedal-power rickshaws was phenomenal: no wonder Dhaka was called the Rickshaw Capital of the World. The place looked almost medieval. But the rickshaws were not the shocking thing.

The Bangladeshi capital was home to 15 million people, making it the eighth largest city in the world. It was also one of the most densely populated, and, when I looked to my left, I could see this for myself. I was staring at perhaps the greatest mass of humanity I'd seen in my life. Known as Kawran Bazaar, thousands of people were crowding around the sprawling fruit and vegetable market, some walking in lines with large bundles on their head, reminding me of leafcutter ants at work, others trying to sell things, but the vast majority crowding around the stalls. Some of the stalls were covered by corrugated metal roofs weighed down with tyres, but most were open air, with produce laid upon the dusty ground. Rickshaws and dilapidated trucks inched their way through the thronging mass while people scurried in all directions. This scene, above all others we'd seen on our trip, brought home to me that we were in the Third World.

"My God," said Angela, joining me. "I thought Delhi was bad…"

She let the statement hang in the air. As we studied the scene in more detail, I could see thin people traipsing about in the dust, and dirty brown dogs patrolling the piles of rubbish at the periphery. I remembered being shown photos of poverty as a child at school; the scene below was exactly that – poverty.

4

After breakfast, we met our guide for the day, a man in his late forties called Asraf. He reminded me a little of Dinesh, our guide in Delhi, especially with his neatly-pressed shirt and thick black moustache. We all shook hands and he led us outside to the car and driver.

The streets of Dhaka were hot and humid, making the smell from the rotting piles of garbage assault our nostrils. We climbed into the back of the car, thankful for its air conditioning, but more or less as soon as we set off, we joined the traffic jam I'd seen from the window. A mob of women in the road was the cause. Some were holding banners, but most were just shouting. One woman was hollering so loudly that her shrill voice invaded the interior of the car.

"There is too much traffic in Dhaka," Asraf stated. "The city was never built for the amount of vehicles it now has. And these demonstrations make things worse."

"What are they protesting about?" asked Angela.

"Low wages – the usual thing. But if everyone protested about low wages, like these garment workers, then the whole city would be on strike."

I looked to my right. Tiny stalls lined the street with the ever-present coils of cables hanging around their awnings. A man carrying a fistful of chickens by their feet wandered past and a woman, wearing a brightly-coloured sari, had a large tray of oranges balanced upon her head. As we moved forward a few metres, we stopped adjacent to a large pile of rubbish. People were poking about in it with sticks trying to find some useful item amongst the stench. Crows and buzzards summed up the bird population, the buzzards circling while the crows scavenged near the meat sellers to fight over scraps of discarded offal. And then, quite suddenly, we passed the protesting women and gathered pace, overtaking the wiry rickshaw drivers pedalling with sudden fury. We were passing through a whirlwind of colour and dust. And people, of course. Unimaginable numbers of people.

5

I asked Asraf about the power cuts in Dhaka. He shook his head and frowned. "They are not good. Every district of the city has a power cut at a different time of the day. Each power cut lasts for two hours, then comes back on for two hours, and so on. Where I live, with my wife and two daughters, the power goes off when my daughters need to sleep. It is too hot in their room because we can't power the fans. They have to wait until the power comes back on at 1am to sleep. The next morning they are too tired to go to school."

Asraf told us that the power cuts were due to power being redirected to fertiliser plants in the north. "The plants are part of the rice farming industry. But a question many people are asking, me included, is why the government is not building more power plants? It seems a logical solution. But as it stands, everyone in Dhaka suffers the power cuts. It is a crazy situation."

I felt guilty at the way I'd complained to Angela about the power going off in the hotel the previous evening. First, the lights had flickered, and then the power had gone down, causing an immediate and startling darkness. The air conditioning had ceased to work, and our charging phones then beeped in annoyance. About a minute later, a deep rumbling noise came from somewhere within, as the hotel's generators kicked into action. Everything came back on, a luxury most of the population of Dhaka did not have.

6

Old Dhaka was a complex web of narrow streets and alleys, crammed with people, shops and rickshaws. Crumbling paintwork, crisscrossing wires and colourful Bengali script made up the sides of the warren. Fly posters of politicians were everywhere too, some of them so sun-scorched that they had turned blue. Our car negotiated its way through one such alleyway towards our first stop of the tour.

The Dhakeswari Temple is the city's main Hindu place of worship. Its grounds are in the middle of a tight jumble of residential buildings and rusted shop fronts. Dating from the twelfth century, it is a rather small complex, made up of four red and pink Shiva temples spread across the uneven and dusty ground. A few statues and engravings add some interest, but the most interesting feature was a small man-made lake overlooked by some decrepit, grey concrete buildings, all blackened by grime. The only colour came from the bright fabric hanging at the windows. Asraf told us the buildings were apartment blocks and were less than ten years old.

At the lake's edge, an old man was washing his clothes in the murky water, so absorbed in his task that he didn't notice the three of us staring. I turned around to gaze at the threadbare shrines. For such an important temple, there didn't seem many.

"Most were destroyed," said Asraf, "during the Bangladesh Liberation War of 1971. Almost half the temple buildings were blown up or battered to the ground."

"Why?"

"Because Pakistani troops from Islamabad didn't like Hindus. And they didn't just destroy temples like this: all across East Pakistan – as my country was called back then – Hindu homes and businesses were painted with yellow 'H's, and then later burned to the ground. Schools and universities were robbed and looted, and a quarter of a million Hindu women were raped, often ending up as sex slaves in army camps. It was a nightmarish time in my country's history, and, by the end of the war, hundreds of thousands of people lay dead, some say millions. It was genocide, plain and simple."

We all stared at the shrines, not saying anything for a good while. There was nothing to say.

7

After a quick visit to an old and stained pink Mughal complex called Lalbagh Fort, we set off through the streets again. "See that building there," said Asraf, suddenly becoming animated, "it is Dhaka Central Jail."

We looked at a large three-storey prison. A tall wall surrounded its grimy yellow main building, presumably to thwart escape attempts.

"It used to be full of corrupt government officials," Asraf told us. "When Bangladesh gained independence in 1971, everyone was excited because they thought things would change for the better. We were promised trustworthy leaders and an end to corruption – something that had dogged the country for many years. Ordinary people, such as my mother and father, had big hopes for Bangladesh…" Asraf's monologue suddenly stopped. The car was slowing down and pulling over to the side of the road. After conferring with the driver for a moment, Asraf turned to us. "The car is overheating. We need to stop for a short while."

While the driver got out, opening the bonnet to let off steam, Asraf continued with his tale. "But like many countries, our hopes were short lived. The new government became as corrupt as the old one. People who were suffering before were still suffering. When Bangladesh became riddled with famine, the government did not care; they did not lift a finger."

Outside, the driver was busy pouring cold water into the radiator, causing more steam to billow out around the engine compartment. Without the cool of the air-conditioner, though, the heat inside the car became unbearable, so we all stepped outside. The street was busy with fruit stands, the beginnings of a market. A man sitting under a black umbrella, toiling away on an old sewing machine, looked up and stared. People in the market did too. Within seconds, we became the centre of attention.

"Eventually," said Asraf, ignoring the stares, "the people decided enough was enough. They were sick of the corruption and tired of the people at the top living like kings while they slept in the dirt. My father was one of the people demanding change, and I remember how angry he used to be at home, saying that unless things changed then we would have to leave for India. But things did change. Some government officials were arrested and thrown into prison – the one we passed earlier – and another government was formed. Bangladesh had a chance of righting all the wrongs from the past – an excellent opportunity – but it was not to be. The new government was just as bad, and all the corrupt officials were released from their cells and allowed back into their positions."

While Asraf talked to the driver, Angela and I wandered over to a white bearded man sitting near a rectangle of cloth. He was surrounded by bunches of bananas. I bought five and they were ridiculously cheap. The lack of tourists in Bangladesh meant that the locals were not hiking their prices yet. The man even gave me some change, which I waved away.

Steam was still escaping from the engine when we returned with our booty. A few bystanders had gathered around the engine, but at a discreet distance. I offered Angela a banana but she didn't want one, and neither did Asraf or the driver, and so I ate mine alone. People on the street watched me eat it and I nodded, miming that it was a good banana. Most of them smiled. Ten minutes later, the car's engine had cooled sufficiently to allow us to proceed.

8

The Sitara Mosque was next door to a boys' school. It was breaktime, so as soon as we got out of the car, a crowd ran up to the wire fence hollering, laughing and leering. Asraf took us past the boys to the gate of the mosque, but found it locked. "I don't know why it is closed," said Asraf apologetically, "Because yesterday it was open and the day before that too. I don't know what to say."

We told him not to worry, and stood at the railings. Instead of towering minarets, the Sitara Mosque featured a series of white domes decorated with dark blue stars. It was quite beautiful, especially with the topical palms and large star-shaped bathing pool in front of it.

"That building there," Asraf said, pointing at a broken down building in dire need of repair behind us, "is one of the oldest in Dhaka. Soon it will be pulled down to make way for residential quarters." I looked at it. With a bit of restoration, it would look fine. It seemed a shame to pull it down to make way for apartment blocks. "But the owner doesn't care about the historical importance of the building, only for the money he can make. In his eyes, if he keeps the building, he will be a poor man and his family will starve. If he sells the building to a land developer, he will be very rich. It is a simple equation for him."

Back in the car, with our driver worried about overheating the engine, we drove at a slower pace. When we stopped at a traffic jam, a young woman holding a baby approached my window. When she had our attention, she held the baby by its midriff, showing me the naked infant's behind. Angela gasped. The poor thing was in need of medical attention because, instead of just a bare bottom, it had a two-inch long, half-inch thick, bright red protrusion emanating from its nether regions.

The next stop was, in my opinion, the best part of the tour. The River Sadarghat, though smelly and muddy, was the lifeblood of old Dhaka. The busy boat terminal was a feast for the eyes and an assault on the nose. Triple-decked ferries, docked along the side of the jetty, were gently bobbing on the swell, while small wooden boats, under the control of single oarsmen, plied their trade in between. The God-awful smell was coming from the waves of rubbish surrounding the jetty supports, a moving mass of rotting vegetables, offal and palm leaves. It suddenly occurred to me that the boat terminal reminded me of Venice, albeit after the Italians had ransacked the place and left rotting turnips everywhere.

A few enterprising pedlars had set up stalls along the gangways, most of them selling tiny cups of tea. Asraf decided he wanted one, so while he waited at the nearest stand, Angela and I wandered to the end of the concourse to watch some large boats offloading large sacks of spices, nuts and produce to the waiting divisions of rickshaws.

"This is amazing," I said. "Really and truly amazing. Maybe the best thing I've seen on this trip."

Angela didn't reply.

I dropped my gaze to a boat bobbing about in the water below. A boatman was having a cigarette break at the stern of his wooden vessel. He looked up and nodded. I nodded back and smiled. Asraf appeared by our side with his small cup of tea. "So tell me," he asked, "what you think of the river?"

"I love it." I said.

"Really?"

"Absolutely. I think it's because it's so different from what we're used to. So colourful…so alive."

The boatman finished his cigarette and threw it into the water. Another small wooden boat sailed past him. Its passenger was a woman wearing a red and orange sari holding an umbrella to keep the sun at bay. Asraf said, "Sometimes I like to ask visitors to Dhaka what they see through their eyes, because mine are old and have seen things many times." He caught sight of something in the water. "But sometimes even my eyes see things I don't understand – would you look at that?"

Two naked boys aged about ten were swimming in the murky brown water next to one of the large rusted ferries. They were having a whale of a time, but Asraf was shaking his head. "If you paid me one hundred thousand taka, I would not swim in that water. The diseases in there, I can only imagine."

I took one last lingering look at the life and energy going on around the Sadarghat River and turned away. It was time for the last stop of the tour.

9

Ahsan Manzil, otherwise known as the Pink Palace due to the colour of its exterior, dated from 1872 and was a large, colonial-style building surrounded by a nice garden nestling on the banks of the river. Inside the palace was a museum that housed photos, thrones, old coins and lots more besides, and I could tell Asraf was going to take great delight in showing them all to us. Fifteen minutes into his tour, with Angela and me traipsing after him, the power went off, sending the already dim interior into near darkness.

"This is absurd," exclaimed Asraf, cutting short his spiel about the glory days of old Dhaka, and in particular when the prominent Dhaka Naweb family had resided inside the palace. His face furrowed into bitterness. "Another power cut! Museums should have generators for such a thing."

Inwardly I was overjoyed, and I knew Angela was too. We'd managed to avoid museums on our trip so far, for the simple reason that we found them dull. One display looked much like the next, and after seeing a broken pot in one museum, we didn't really need to see another in a different museum. But I did feel bad for Asraf. He clearly wanted to show us more of his country's heritage, but with the power cut due to last for another couple of hours, he had no choice but to cut short the visit. We walked out to the car, with our guide bemoaning the power situation in Dhaka all the way. "I will reduce my fee accordingly," he said as we set off driving again. "You should not have to pay for the failings of my government."

An hour later (after suffering yet another overheated engine stoppage) we pulled up near the hotel. We paid Asraf the full amount and gave the driver a healthy tip too. Both men thanked us and we all said goodbye. It was time for something to eat.

10

Lunch was served in the hotel restaurant. I was especially taken with the can of local Bangladeshi beer than appeared on my table. It was called Hunter Lager, and the can looked suspiciously like Foster's Lager. It had the same blue can with white vertical lettering and a golden ring around the big red letter. Instead of having an F for Foster's, it had a capital H. I loved it. As we tucked into some grilled fish, a man in a suit came over and asked if everything was okay. It was, and we told him so.

"That is good to hear," the man said, smiling. He introduced himself as the hotel manager, and went on to ask us other questions about the hotel, the staff and the service we had received.

"All good," I said, taking another slurp of Hunter's. "Really nice hotel. No complaints."

The man seemed happy with that news and excused himself. When he was out of earshot, I leaned in towards Angela. "You never get that in England, or even in Qatar."

"That's because there are no other Westerners staying here. In fact, I reckon we might be the only Westerners in Dhaka right now."

I nodded. "You are probably right."

After lunch, I felt it was time to tackle the streets of Dhaka by ourselves. Angela told me that she was going to stay in the hotel to pack, explaining that she was not really that bothered about seeing anything else in the Bangladeshi capital.

"Anyone would think you didn't like it," I said.

"It's not that; I'm just tired out. We've been on the go for weeks. How many different hotels have we stayed in? I just can't face any more. Plus I'm sick of being stared at all the time. You go off for a wander; I'll stay and pack the suitcases."

And so, armed with a Lonely Planet map of downtown Dhaka, a bottle of water and a cap to cover my head, I left Angela to her packing and set forth on a solo adventure.

11

I stepped into the heat and dripping humidity with a mission to have a drink at the Sheraton Hotel, which, according to the map, was two kilometres away. At first things went remarkably well. I avoided the large potholes that seemed to be a fixture of Dhaka's pavements, and I managed to sidestep most of the rotting vegetables and black puddles that dotted my path. I even succeeded in crossing a railway line, which, only moments before had seen a large locomotive juddering past. As soon as it disappeared, the people of Dhaka began using the tracks as a footpath again.

I turned along a street and found myself the centre of attention again. Auto-rickshaw repair shacks made up most of the business along both sides of the road. Men who, only a few minutes previously, had been whacking bits of metal now stopped to gawp. None of the looks suggested any malice, of course, only blatant curiosity. *What is the white man doing wandering down this road when he clearly does not own an auto-rickshaw? Why is the white man dripping like a wreck and blotching his clothes? Where is the white man going, because there is nothing along this street for him?*

After almost falling down a large hole, I consulted my map and then took a left-hand turn, hoping I was going in the right direction. To be honest, though, I didn't have a clue where I was. There were no landmarks to take bearings from, no street signs I could read, and I didn't want to ask anyone because I knew they would not be able to understand me. After a few hundred metres or so, I looked at the map again, but decided it was more of a hindrance than a help and so shoved it deep into my pocket. With about thirty pairs of eyes staring at me, I drained my bottle of water in one go and shook my head in consternation.

I considered retracing my steps, but the thought of walking past all the mechanics stopped me. Instead, I trudged along in the heat, hoping against hope I would stumble across something recognisable. My thoughts were broken when I spied a man crawling in front of me. One of his legs was not in working order, at least judging by the way it trailed after his body. Horribly, his other leg was worse. It was bent upwards at an unnatural angle, causing the man to wriggle using only his elbows for propulsion. I passed him, wondering how he could possibly live like that, and then returned and dropped a few taka banknotes in front of him. I didn't look to see if he picked them up; I was already turning another corner.

I was hoping for the Sheraton to appear like a mirage, but with every minute taking me deeper into Dhaka, I had to admit defeat. I stuck my arm into the road and flagged down a rickshaw. One stopped within seconds.

"The Sheraton Hotel," I said as clearly as possible to the driver, but I might as well have spoken Latin. The man stared at me in confusion. Wiping at my brow, I fished out the map and pointed. He looked at it but wobbled his head.

"SHER-A-TON HO-TEL," I repeated to blank eyes. Just as I was about to burst into tears, another man approached. At first I thought he was trying to commandeer my ride, but he ended up being my saviour. "English?" he asked

I nodded heavily.

By now, there were a hundred eyes upon me. The whole street was watching the exchange, especially now that I had stopped a rickshaw. I wiped at my brow again, sending a cascade of wetness to the ground. The new man, wearing a cheap suit and trainers, was speaking to the rickshaw driver. I waited with a rising sense of hope.

"He...not know...where you go...?" the newcomer said in broken but perfectly understandable English.

"I want to go to the Sheraton Hotel."

"Ah..., Sheraton. I know."

The man relayed the information to the rickshaw driver, who nodded and gestured that I should climb aboard his craft. I thanked my saviour, who smiled and walked away. A moment later, I was sitting in the back of a contraption designed exclusively for not being in the thick of motorised traffic and, for the next thirty minutes, I sweltered in the heat while my man pedalled his way to the Sheraton. How he did this hour after hour, day after day, in the heat and dust, I had no idea.

When we pulled up outside the hotel, the rickshaw driver held up four fingers. I didn't know whether he meant forty taka (30p) or four hundred (£3), so I passed him a five hundred note. The man waved it away, moving his finger and thumb together: *smaller.* I passed him a 40-note and he nodded and pocketed it. Because of his honesty, I gave him the four hundred as well. His eyes lit up; he didn't know what to do, but I was already climbing out of the rickshaw into the grounds of the Sheraton.

12

The Sheraton was fancy. It had a large café in the foyer, where I found a seat. Like most other Sheratons I'd been in, Dhaka's also had a gift shop, but instead of rustic souvenirs, it sold pirated DVDs.

I texted Angela, saying that I'd arrived unscathed, and she replied by telling me that she'd finished packing and was about to hit the hotel gym. I ordered a coffee and a can of cola, downing the latter in twenty seconds, much to the amusement of the waiters. As I sipped on my coffee, I began to read an English-language newspaper called the *Dhaka Tribune* that someone had left on my table. The main story was about power cuts, complaining, as Asraf had done, about the lack of government funding for the city's power infrastructure. Another story described how a young mother had strangled her eight-month-old baby daughter to death because the man she was intending to marry had found out about the child and had called the wedding off. Also making the news were reports of fires all over the city. Dhaka, it seemed, was a veritable tinderbox, and one had gutted over a hundred shanty houses, their occupants rendered immediately homeless. The strangest story was on the back page. According to the article, plainclothes policemen were now patrolling the exits to every girls' school in Dhaka. Male 'delinquents' had been harassing (or as the newspaper phrased it, *eye-teasing*) the girls to the point where some had committed suicide.

I finished my coffee and pondered how to get back to the hotel. My map was clearly as useless as my navigating skills; therefore walking was out of the question. I decided the best course of action was to get the lobby staff to order me a taxi. While I was waiting for it to arrive, I decided to sit on a wall just outside the entrance. After a minute or so of staring, a young bellboy approached. Witnessing this bold move, a hotel security guard decided to come over too. The two men stood next to me, smiling broadly. The bellboy spoke first. "Where are you from?" he asked.

"England, United Kingdom."

Both men smiled even more. I was waiting for a follow-up question, but none came. Instead of returning to their posts, though, the pair remained next to me, studying me as I shifted position on the wall. When neither man said anything further, I felt compelled to break the silence. "What job do you do at the hotel?" I asked the bellboy, even though the answer was obvious.

He appeared nonplussed and so I rephrased my question. "What do you do here at the hotel?

"Ah!" he said, "you mean duty, sir?"

I nodded encouragingly.

"It is from 1pm till 10pm, sir!"

I nodded thoughtfully. "I see." I wondered what to ask the security guard, but just then, my car arrived and I took my leave. Both men shook my hand and watched me go.

13

"How was your little adventure?" asked Angela.

I told her about getting lost, seeing the man crawling on the ground, and about my rickshaw journey to the Sheraton. I told her about the two workers at the hotel and I told her that, yes, I had enjoyed my adventure.

"But was it worth all the effort? I mean, you were gone ages."

"Totally worth it. I love Bangladesh. It makes me feel alive being here, more so than in any of the other places we've been to on this trip."

Angela looked at me oddly; I could tell she thought differently. But in Dhaka, I had discovered something new and exciting. It wasn't a temple or an ancient monument, or a skyscraper reflecting in the sun, it was *life*. Life abounded in the purest of forms along Dhaka's brown riverbanks and bazaars, life whistled past on rickshaws and wooden boats. Life stared out from the dingy interior of a rickshaw repair shop and life congregated on every street corner to barter, to sell or to hold protest banners. And the fact that tourists had not yet discovered this wealth of life, this richness of colour (as they had in Delhi, Kathmandu and Colombo), meant the city was still raw and exciting. My only wish was that we were staying longer. The man at the airport had been correct: two days was not anywhere near long enough to enjoy the fruits of Bangladesh.

Angela and I spent the remainder of the evening looking back at the photos we had taken throughout our trip. Memories came flooding back to the fore. An Indian dance show in Delhi, a fabulous white temple in Agra, a boy on stilts in Kathmandu and an elephant with a huge penis in Sri Lanka: all part of a rich visual tapestry that had made our trip so special.

"We *are* lucky," said Angela again. She was looking at a photo of a Kerala sunset. It brought back recollections of drinking Kingfisher Beer from a cup and trying to decipher an unbreakable crossword. She flicked through to Sri Lanka: to Kandy, Galle and Beruwala, then switched the camera off and packed it away in its special compartment.

"So that's it, then," I said. "Finished."

Angela was taking the passports out of the hotel safe, worried that we might forget them otherwise. It was time to say goodbye to the Indian Subcontinent once and for all, and there was no better place to do it than in the centre of chaos, crowds and colour: Dhaka, capital of Bangladesh.

Top row: The lifeblood of Old Dhaka – The River Sadarghat; Me posing in Dhaka
Middle row: The local Hunter lager looks suspiciously like Foster's! A banana seller in the old town
Bottom row: A trio of rickshaw drivers pedal in harmony; The Sitara Mosque;

If you enjoyed reading Crowds, Colour, Chaos then perhaps you will like the author's other travel books. All are available on Amazon.

The Red Quest
Flashpacking through Africa
The Balkan Odyssey
Temples, Tuk-tuks and Fried Fish Lips
Panama City to Rio de Janeiro
Bite Size Travel in North America
Crowds, Colour, Chaos

Visit www.theredquest.com for more details.

Praise for Jason Smart's travel books:

The Red Quest

"One of the best books I have read in ages. Like the author, I have always been fascinated with Russia and behind the Iron Curtain, I have been to many Eastern European countries and this book brought back fond memories. I am now inspired to head off to the 'Stans, especially Turkmenistan. If you are looking for an easy to read travel book, this book is for you."

"Had a great time reading this book. I must admit I am a bit of a Sovietophile, and reading about all these amazing places was a treat. I too would one day love to organize my very own red quest and visit all these places."

"Jason Smart is a great writer who brings his light touch to a part of the world that can be stodgy and humourless. Great entertaining read for armchair travellers but also a good source of insights for anyone planning to travel to Russia."

"I found this a fascinating read about countries I'd only gazed out of the window at 30,000 ft of a commercial airliner on my way to more popular destinations. The Red Quest is an easy and humorous read which inspires and motivates one to get off one's derrière and consider travel to countries off the main frame."

"As a keen traveller myself, I enjoy reading tales told by fellow like-minded adventurers. This book is particularly enjoyable as it gives a little bit of background, adds in some humour and gives a realistic portrayal of what it would be like to visit some of these off-the-beaten-track countries. After reading this book I certainly feel inspired to find out more about places like Turkmenistan or Kyrgyzstan."

"This book is a real gem and a must read for any lover of travel and history. Jason opens doors that most of us wouldn't even dare knock on. This book is an account of his travels through former Soviet-era countries, which range from the obscure to the downright unknown. The pace of his account is fast, and the scenes are brought to life by the author's acute ability to capture a slice of life in places like a jailhouse in Kyrgyzstan, a torture museum in Bratislava, or a market in a breakaway country east of Moldova."

"I'm an American woman who has always had a fascination with the former USSR. Ever since an elementary school project where I was to report on my ancestors, I've been hooked. This present account of out there was right up my alley."

"I have spent 8 months in the former Soviet countries and it was interesting for me to compare my feelings about those countries with somebody else's. Just finished reading the book (couldn't even stop in the middle of it!). Jason Smart brings so much realistic and priceless information about all ex-USSR and ex-communist party countries with plenty of humour. Reading his book is like listening

to your old friend talking about his adventures. When I travelled to Russia, the first question I was asked at Domodedovo airport was exactly the same - "Zis your first time in Russia?"

Flashpacking through Africa

"The most compelling aspect of this book for me was the way in which Mr Smart balanced the general humour and lightness of style with the more sensitive aspects that travelling to these sorts of places necessarily brings up. His style is personable, pulling no punches, direct and with many insights. I have only been to South Africa, of the countries mentioned, and it is such an engaging tale that it definitely leaves you looking up flights!"

"This book is not the usual type of travel book I enjoy reading. Just for a change the book is about a couple who travel through Africa but instead of back packing, let's rough it attitude, they decide to stay in nice, almost top of the range hotels. It's a lovely book to read although some of the history of some countries in Africa leaves a lot to be desired. Amusing in parts, very thought provoking in others."

"Jason Smart is an excellent writer and I thoroughly enjoyed exploring Africa with him."

"Nice light style and good eye for detail, as well as a good line in dry humour. Excellent for the armchair traveller to catch the lighter side of Africa without getting bogged down in neediness. Well worth a read."

"I never intend to travel to most of the countries that Mr. Smart visited, but he has given the armchair traveller a delightful dip into exotic places that would remain hidden had he not given us a realistic glimpse into places few of us will ever venture. What I

especially appreciated was his very middle-class approach to travel. Having read Lonely Planet guides of fleabag-level treks, or, worse, packaged tours in which one never actually mingles with people or ventures out on foot, the Smarts were the sort of travellers my husband and I tend to be – maximizing limited time experiencing the highlights up close and on a reasonable budget. I feel I have a better sense of the distinct geographical features and cultures of the countries they visited and learned things that both saddened me and gave me more appreciation for these African countries."

"I enjoyed this book immensely. It has good tips for travelling in specific African countries. It was funny and informative at the same time. I recommend this book to anyone who likes to travel."

"This author gets it, he provides a no-nonsense eye into his tour of Africa and provides the reader with a full experience. If you are someone who is itching to tour Africa yourself, this will be a priceless guide. Unlike the other passive guides, Flashpacking through Africa provides a side story of someone who's been there and done it all. Full of rich detail and immersive experiences. Highly recommended."

The Balkan Odyssey

"I enjoyed this book very much. It covered countries that I have not been to or read about before. There was enough history to make it interesting but not so much that I skipped any."

"A breezy account of two blokes from Manchester on a whistle-stop tour of the Balkans. One likes museums, the other one doesn't. As an Englishman who lives in one of the ex-Yugoslav republics (Slovenia), I'm familiar with the places described, so the blokey Englishmen-abroad account is refreshing."

"I enjoyed this offering from Jason Smart. He travelled around the Balkans and gave a bit of history of the areas as he went, some not at all pleasant and hard to stomach. It made a change to read about a place, warts and all."

"Thoroughly enjoyed revisiting places I visited in the Balkans three years ago on an Explore Holiday. I've yet to go to Albania but Jason made me want to visit the bits of the Balkans we didn't visit!"

"Easy read, likeable author. Explains about former Yugoslavia in a nutshell. Ideal for a first timer about Balkans…"

"I love books like this, as they are a nice quick and easy read on a subject that I love (travel). I enjoyed his witty writing, detailing a whistle stop tour of the former Yugoslavia, not forgetting of course Albania, which had to be included as Smart and his travelling companion Michael had to travel through Albania to get to some of the other countries they visited. Smart gently pokes fun at his travelling companion who is walking satnav with a love of museums, unlike Smart himself who has not a cultural bone in his body. Somehow they get along without killing each other, which is sadly more than can be said for those who inhabit these former Yugoslav states."

Temples, Tuk-tuks and Fried Fish Lips

"A seven-week trip travelling to various Far East locations, providing a little bit on each stop, because that was what the trip was, 2 or 3 days in each location. I enjoyed the author's writing style (in my case, I often TRY to read someone's travel book, but get quickly bored by their writing style, and give up). I kept reading right to the end, and would definitely read another travel book by Jason Smart. He is down to earth, doesn't take on hoity-

toity airs, doesn't whine or complain, can laugh at his own misadventures during the trip."

"Having visited most of the places mentioned in this book I enjoyed travelling the road again on every page. Super!"

"I have read three travel books by this author and enjoyed them all, his style is so straight forward and although he does not rough it, he still has quite a few uncomfortable experiences. There is a lot of humour in his accounts as well, and this was a book that I did not want to put down. By reading this I almost felt I was with them on the journey."

"I've read a few of Jason Smart's books and they never fail to engage me in his travels. This time he and Angela are on their travels around Bangkok, Bali and Borneo. The food is always a major part of travel and to be honest a lot of it leaves a lot to be desired - hence the title of the book! The authors amusing fixation with a loo seat in Tokyo is funny... just how many times can you need to flush a loo? I really enjoyed this book. I feel as if I've been on the trip myself. Great stuff."

Panama City to Rio de Janeiro

"I would recommend this book to anyone who enjoys travel writing books and likes to read about people and places often off the beaten track. There is no putting up of tents and breaking down of bikes, as the author and his wife stay in hotels – albeit some leaving a lot to be desired. The local transport they used did bring all kind of problems at times and some of the encounters often described by the author were simply hilarious. The book is very easy to read and takes you to so many fascinating places, a very hard book to put down."

"Panama City to Rio de Janeiro is a great travel book for anyone planning on travelling to South America. I have been considering vacationing in South America for some time and this book convinced me that it would be a great vacation spot."

"Warts and all, Jason tells it as it is. I felt I was on the buses with him and his wife as they travelled from place to place. Some areas they visited were a bit better than others. Some maybe they shouldn't have gone to at all. I read a lot of travel books...this one I will read again in the future."